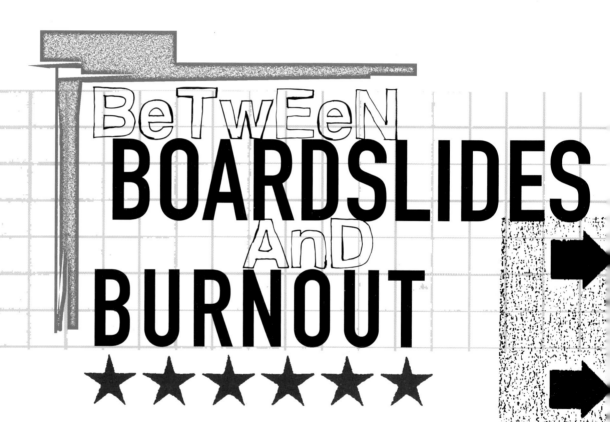

BeTwEeN
BOARDSLIDES
AnD
BURNOUT

★★★★★★

2000
2001

BeTwEeN
BOARDSLIDES
AnD
BURNOUT

MY NOTES FROM THE ROAD

tony hawk

ReganBooks
An Imprint of HarperCollinsPublishers

HarperCollins books may be purchased for educational, business, or sales promotional use. For information please write: Special Markets Department, HarperCollins Publishers Inc., 10 East 53rd Street, New York, NY 10022.

FIRST EDITION

Designed by Platinum Design, Inc., NYC

Library of Congress Cataloging-in-Publication Data

Hawk, Tony.
    Between boardslides and burnout : my notes from the road / by Tony Hawk.-- 1st ed.
      p.cm.
    ISBN 0-06-008631-9
      1. Hawk, Tony--Journeys. 2. Skateboarders--United States--Biography. I. Title.

GV859.813.H39 A29 2002
796.21'092--dc21
[B]

                                                                    2002068105

02 03 04 05 06 QW 10 9 8 7 6 5 4 3 2 1

Riley doing a bed-to-bed transfer.

INTRODUCTION:
welcome to my world

LIFE ON THE ROAD IS A WORLD UNTO ITSELF.

THERE IS NO WAY TO DESCRIBE THE REALITY OF BEING IN A DIFFERENT CITY EVERY DAY, SLEEPING IN A NEW BED EVERY NIGHT, AND SHARING THE CLOSE COMPANY OF ONLY A FEW OTHERS ALONG THE WAY.

It is in turns exciting, grueling, glamorous, disgusting, tiring, comical, stressful, and shocking—but it is never boring. I have been touring regularly since I was sixteen years old, and I am well aware of the jaded perspective from which we (the lucky travelers who tour at others' expenses) view the world. We have a sense of immunity from normal rules and an unspoken creed that whatever happens on the road is just part of the game. I never forget that skating is what got me here, so that is always the priority when touring. You can't live too excessively when you're required to put on daily athletic performances.

As a husband and a father of three boys, I find touring all the more surreal. My life shifts from normal spousal duties at home—like fixing breakfast for the kids, taking them to school, attending parent-teacher conferences, taking out the trash, paying bills, waiting in line at the DMV, reading *Hop on Pop*, and watching *SpongeBob SquarePants*—to flying in private jets, performing in front of thousands of people, getting VIP treatment at restaurants and clubs, and having everything paid for by someone else. Neither lifestyle allows sufficient sleep, but I am completely thankful to have both. I love my family life and the normalcy that defines it, and I realize that the road's carefree glamour is short-lived. Striking a healthy balance between being home and being away is the biggest challenge of my life. I've become very selective about which events or projects I get involved with. My wife, Erin, has an amazing ability to keep our family grounded in reality while accepting that my time away is a mandatory aspect of what I do for a living. I bring my family along whenever possible, but often my schedule is not conducive to hauling around three kids. It's not fun for them and is more stressful than enjoyable for my wife and me. My oldest son, Riley, is an avid skater and a well-seasoned traveler, so he often joins me on trips (depending on his school absentee status). It is refreshing to view new places and experiences through his eyes, because I often forget to simply relax and be a tourist amid all the hype.

I realize that this dual lifestyle could all come to a screeching halt (due to injury, popularity decline, or an ultimatum from home) at some point, and I am thankful for everything I have experienced so far. I never imagined that riding empty swimming pools as a kid would become a career, and I could only dream that my career would be this much fun.

The following is part of a longer journal that I have kept throughout my travels, usually written on the flight home. I've tried to be selective about the entries, choosing only those that involve some sort of milestone, interesting anecdote, or lesson. It covers the past two years, which have been among the craziest in terms of scheduling and prospects. As you read, a couple of patterns should emerge: first, you'll discover that skateboarding as a career is much more work than you ever imagined; second, you should be able to trace a steady increase in skateboarding's recognition and respectability. You can also see how my life as a skater has been a catalyst for many other opportunities like work in movies and television, and invitations to many different fund-raisers and events.

The strangest part about garnering this much fame is that I never skated in hopes of being a celebrity. Skaters were outcasts when I was growing up, and a skating career wasn't even an option. There was no money to be made. Everything has changed (some argue that it has for the worst, most agree it's for the better), and I am proud to be considered a professional skateboarder at age thirty-four, honored to have had so many opportunities, and grateful that people have finally accepted skateboarding for its positive aspects. So here it is: life on the road, swaying between board-slides and burnout, and having a blast during the process.

THinGs
I HAVE LEARNED FROM EXTENSIVE TRAVELING:

Airline ticket agents are capable of almost anything (flight upgrades, waiving fees, rerouting, rescheduling, and so forth), but it all depends on your attitude and their mood at the time. They're also capable of keeping you from making your flight.

Checking out of a hotel is a waste of time. They know when you're scheduled to leave, they already have your credit card and address, and they'll mail you an itemized receipt if there are any charges in question.

Once you get to fly first class internationally, you never want to go back to coach.

Artsy hotels have the most beautiful clientele (all Ian Schrager and Peter Morton hotels, for example).

You can almost always use your own headphones to watch in-flight movies. Sometimes the sound only comes out of one side, but it's worth not being scammed for an extra four dollars when you've probably already paid hundreds to be on the flight. Rarely do flight attendants take notice, as long as you plug in just as the movie is starting.

There are some exceptional restaurants that have more than one location these days, including P.F. Chang's, The Cheesecake Factory, Nobu, Romano's Macaroni Grill, Ruth's Chris Steak House, China Grill, and Wahoo's Fish Taco.

While flying, wear clothes that may be suitable or comfortable for more than one day in case your luggage is delayed. Also be sure to carry any absolute necessities with you, rather than checking them, for the same reason.

Frequent flier miles are invaluable, if for no other reason than being able to wait in a shorter check-in line.

One-third of all flight attendants comment about skating down the aisle when they see you carrying a skateboard onto an airplane.

Laptop batteries never last as long as they're supposed to, so bring at least one backup on a flight if you expect to watch an entire DVD.

There are too many Starbucks. (In fact, there are two directly across the street from each other in many cities.)

Eating in Europe is more of an event than a necessity. Waiters never check up on you, and the quest for a bill is strenuous. If a Euro friend invites you out to dinner, expect it to last at least two hours.

Jet lag is only a major issue when flying over the Atlantic.

All crowds, regardless of culture, love inverts, McTwists, and big airs—just like in the eighties.

Dial-up internet access is seriously expensive when traveling overseas (even when you have a local access number in the country you're visiting).

My Titanium G4 PowerBook is indispensable, and I should treat it better.

Taping for
Tony Hawk Pro Skater 3.

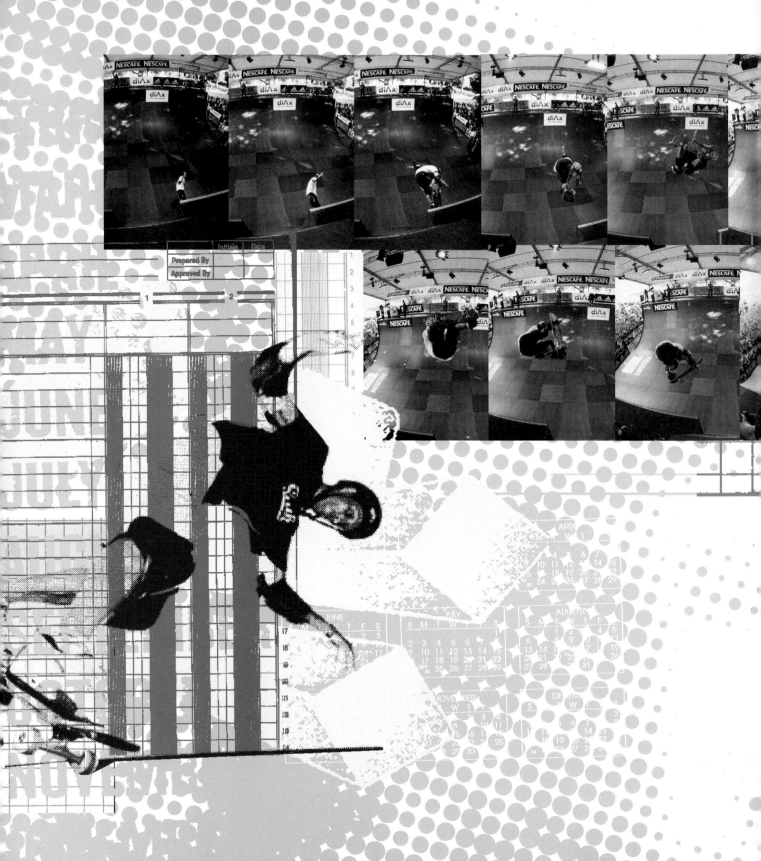

[part 1] 2000

Today was the grand opening of a new public skatepark in Ocean Beach. Andy Macdonald asked if I could come to the pro demo that was scheduled for noon, and I was stoked to skate something new. I didn't expect much, since most city-built parks seem to be small and, in too many cases, poorly designed.

This new park proved me wrong on all accounts—it's huge. The city got its act together and actually consulted skaters on what to build. Too many cities rely on a cement contractor to tell them what skaters like, when the builder has no idea what is functional for skating—that was the disappointing case with the Carlsbad park. Carlsbad is fun, but it should be much better for the money and effort that went into it. Ocean Beach is a blast to skate, although there were too many people nearly colliding at these opening-day festivities.

I took a few good slams trying to transfer out of the big spine bowl into the street course but luckily hurt nobody else in the process of hurting myself. It was very gratifying seeing such a big crowd turn out for a skatepark opening, further confirming skating's general acceptance in our society. We are here to stay, and another permanent city-built skate facility shows the support that we have finally gained. Thank you, San Diego.

Bowls and spines and hips, oh my.

"ThIs NeW pArK pROVeD mE wRoNg On AlL aCcOuNtS— it's huge,,

BIG MAN ON CAMPUS?

MARCH 16, 2000
Jean Farb Middle School: San Diego, California

My sixth grade teacher, Mrs. Lisiak, asked if I would join an event in which alumni come to the school and read books to different classes. She was always my favorite teacher, giving equal chances to every student and always being supportive of my skating. I agreed and met her in the media center at 11 A.M. She told me that she had kept my participation a secret, so as not to draw too much attention. I didn't think this was really necessary, but things got hectic. I read a book to the class about careers in sports, relating all of the baseball/football/basketball facts to what I do. I tried to give anecdotes to keep their wandering attention. I then answered questions from students until the bell rang.

What I thought was the lunch bell was actually the end of the day for the students (it was Thursday, and Thursdays are their short schedule days). Suddenly there was a swarm of kids outside the class door chanting my name and demanding that I come out. I guess word spread throughout the school that I was there. I hung around in the classroom and talked to Mrs. Lisiak for a bit while waiting for the crowd to thin out, but these kids were persistent and didn't seem to lessen in number. Another participant in the reading program happened to be a cop, and he offered to drive his police car up to the door and escort me off the campus. This was becoming a little exaggerated, but there were too many kids to accommodate while I was there.

AS WE DROVE THROUGH THE CAMPUS IN THE CRUISER, KIDS RAN AFTER US, BANGING ON THE WINDOWS (of a cop car!), asking for autographs, and almost getting run over in the process. I sat in the cruiser while the cop's partner got out and drove my car to the nearest shopping center, away from the madness. We swapped in front of Albertson's while a few kids who managed to make it all the way there surrounded my car asking for autographs. Eighteen years ago I was considered an outcast and a nerd in this neighborhood because I skated, and now I needed a police escort to leave it safely.

An Indy nosebone against the Los Angeles skyline.

SKATEPARK OF TAMPA
(S.P.O.T.) MARCH 18, 2000

San Diego, California, to Tampa, Florida

I agreed to do a skate demo for Hanger 19, a shop in San Diego, before realizing that this was the same weekend as the annual Skatepark of Tampa event. I wasn't going to Tampa to compete, but I wanted to go to check out the contest and support the Birdhouse team. I booked a flight to allow me to do both. Jeff Taylor (Adio team manager/darkman) picked me up at 11 A.M. to drive down to the shop. My flight was leaving at 3 P.M., so the schedule was tight.

After the demo, we got some bagel sandwiches to go and pulled up to the airport with thirty minutes to spare. If I decide to quit skating, I could easily get a job at the information counter of the San Diego airport, since I know it all too well. The same goes for LAX, Denver, and Chicago, since they are all United hubs. I checked in and walked straight onto the plane. On the way to Tampa, I managed to catch up on some chapters for a book that Sean Mortimer (Mort) and I are writing. (The deadline is coming way too soon, so I foresee some sleepless nights of editing in the near future.) But I got cut short due to only bringing one PowerBook battery.

Teammates on tour: Bucky and I arriving by boat to a demo on Orlando Citywalk (see ramp in background).

MARCH 19, 2000

I arrived this morning at 12:30 A.M. and woke up at 9 A.M. I headed straight for the park where both the vert event and street finals were scheduled for today.

It is ironic that one of the biggest events in the skate industry in terms of credibility takes place on a mediocre vert ramp. Tampa has had the same vert ramp for more than ten years and the design has been outdated by a bigger standard of ramps. The skatepark has remained in business through skating's toughest times, thanks to the undying devotion of Brian Schaeffer, longtime skater and S.P.O.T. founder. There is an unspoken obligation for the pros to show up for this hardcore skate event. **I'VE NEVER SEEN SO MANY SLAMS** in one vert session as everyone tried to adjust to the smaller transitions. The vert final was more of a contest of who could stay on than who skated best, but a few guys managed to shine.

Earlier, Bucky Lasek informed me that he planned to take one run, nail everything, and walk out, leaving his remaining two runs unskated. This is a legendary move pulled off by Tom Penny, who won the event a few years ago when he had a flawless routine, skated out the door when his time was up, and wasn't seen the rest of the day. Bucky's first run consisted of three bails in a row, so it would have been surprising to see him leave in a blaze of glory. He made his second run, which was very good but not his absolute best. He was forced to take his last run and forego his rockstar ambitions for now. Bob Burnquist had one insane run where he was pulling ridiculous switch variations that only he can do, and he had one recovery from a sketchy landing that didn't seem possible. It was obvious that they were first and second, but it was almost impossible to decide between them. In the end, Bucky won. Other notable performances: Anthony Furlong, who placed third in his first professional event, and Renton Millar, who made kickflip five-0's on every run.

Bucky, Bob, Lance Mountain, Ridge, and I went to lunch, and we came back during the street competition to see Kerry Getz absolutely destroy the place. The loudest crowd approval came when Rick McCrank ollied over the entire pyramid into a frontside nosegrind down the handrail at the end of his run (but after time). Andrew Reynolds took his first two runs but skipped his last due to an exhaustive shooting schedule over the last week. Rodil De Arajo, the wunderkind from Brazil, placed third, because of his unbelievable consistency. McCrank won the best trick event with his nosegrind and placed second in the finals just behind Kerry. This was a true skate event, and it was great to see such a turnout by the crowd as well as the pros.

ESPN'S B3 EVENT MARCH 24, 2000

Lake Havasu, Arizona

My good friend Greg, Jared Prindle (my friend/assistant), and I drove here last night for the ESPN B3 (bikes, boards, and blades—thus the B3) event this weekend. Coincidentally, it was a spring break weekend (okay, no coincidence), so there would be thousands of college students exploring new methods of intoxication. We were mainly an audience to this madness, but it can be great entertainment.

We went to the event site just in time to catch some street practice before the preliminary runs started. The course looked fun, so I decided to skate a little. This turned out to be one of the worst decisions of the weekend.

I skated for about fifteen minutes, testing various obstacles and trying to stay out of the way of the competing pros. I tried to crooked grind a box from a quarterpipe, but it was steeper than I thought. This miscalculation led to my truck missing the ledge and flying over the box with my feet racing to get ahead of my body. As I landed, my knee folded sideways to the outside and I felt a small pop. I instantly felt like I was going to puke—the only other time I've felt queasy from a fall was when I broke my elbow. I sat down and saw a strange protrusion coming out of the side of my knee. I have seen this phenomenon before in my ankle, but it is usually instant swelling from a bad twist and is soft to the touch. This bulge was rock-hard, meaning that my bone was in the wrong place. I got up and my knee felt stiff, but functional. As I walked down the ramp to leave, I felt another pop and realized that it was the bone returning to its normal position. I felt a great sense of relief, but it was scary.

In the evening, Greg, Jared, and I went to witness the infamous spring break festivities, which is basically a thousand people at a club drinking, dancing, and trying not to leave alone. Most of the skaters from the event were there, which always spices up any activity. It was fun to watch for a while, but we eventually got bored and drove home. My knee seemed to be in better shape by the end of the night, but I was still worried.

"the course looked fun, so I decided to skate a little"

Frontside nosegrind, Melbourne, Australia.

Another knee injury, this time while shooting for GQ. I ruined their $1,500 suit in the process and ended up getting cut from the pictorial.

"iT cAn Be GrEaT

eNtErTaInMeNt

On tiptoe, Frontside air, Hamilton, New Zealand.

TOM'S NUTS

MARCH 26, 2000
SPENCER'S BIRTHDAY:
Home, Carlsbad, California

Tom Green on a recent Birdhouse tour: an old-school melon off a jump ramp.

Tom Green called this morning to thank us for the package we sent to him while he was in the hospital, which included a comedy CD, a picture that my son Riley drew, a card from our family, and a bag of nuts. He was diagnosed with testicular cancer two weeks ago, and has undergone two surgeries since then. He had one testicle removed last week and some lymph nodes removed a few days ago. Shocking, especially since he's only twenty-seven years old. He has kept his unbelievable sense of humor throughout this ordeal, and is dedicating a show to the entire process. He is raising awareness about cancer in an entire generation that may have felt immune to any such tragedy.

They did tests on his lymph nodes and the outlook was very good, meaning that he shouldn't have to go through chemotherapy. We are all thankful and amazed at Tom's willpower—he will attend the Oscars this evening (he was released from the hospital this morning) with his girlfriend, Drew Barrymore. I'm sure that the nut and ball jokes will be flying off the hook. It shows great character to be faced with such a dilemma and still have the courage to make fun of it.

Otherwise, Spencer's birthday went well. A houseful of kids is a lesson in patience.

6

Spencer and his Peanuts posse.

OCCUPATION: AUTHOR

MARCH 30, 2000
New York City

Erin and I flew in last night, since today I was a presenter at the ReAct Take Action Awards banquet.

From there, Sarah Hall, my publicist, and I had a meeting with ReganBooks to discuss our current book project, which is still unnamed. I am pushing for *Occupation: Skateboarder,* but it is a little plain. The meeting went well. I have a lot of confidence in ReganBooks.

Writing a book always seemed like a noble experience in which you could come to terms with your past and really understand the evolution of becoming who you are. There is a taste of that, but mostly it's a lot of *work.* Mort and I have been poring over chapters the last two months, and any new idea becomes another two weeks of research and writing. Let's just say that this book will be thorough, but the deadline is closing in fast. As I type this, I have four chapters waiting to be edited and trick explanations to finish (eight in total). Pictures are an entirely different can of worms. I think the deadline is supposed to be April first . . .

Titanium G4: my one constant companion.

NO TIME FOR ILLNESS

APRIL 5, 2000
Carlsbad, California, to Hartford, Connecticut

My knee is definitely getting better, but it aches sporadically. I skated yesterday for the first time since I wrecked it in Arizona. Kneeslides were a struggle, but it worked. I had to shoot ads for Quiksilver and there were deadlines to meet, so Grant Brittain, my old skatepark manager who is now a famous skate photographer, obliged and we got a few sequences. I don't have the confidence in my knee to go through the motions of learning something new, so we shot tricks I could already do. To make it interesting, I did each trick (ollie five, ollie to bluntslide, frontside cab, and a gay twist heelflip body varial) over the six-foot channel at Mission Valley. I tried to do a backside pop shove-it, but the wind was not cooperating.

I think I'm getting sick. I woke up today with serious aches, but I assumed it was from skating so much yesterday after being out of commission. That may have contributed, but it's more than just skate aches. I feel like every motion is a task and my head is going to droop into oblivion. The last time I felt like this was during an Australian tour in 1996, and I stayed sick for several weeks afterward. I don't have time for sickness these days . . . Now, where did I put the Advil?

APRIL 6, 2000

I got up at 6:30 A.M. after a hopeless night of tossing and turning (the NyQuil didn't work as well as I'd hoped). My call time was at 7:30 at ESPN headquarters. They are shooting a bunch of *Sports-Center* commercials this week, so there are at least three crews working at once. My first job was pretending to be asleep when someone makes a prank phone call to me. It is supposed to be someone at *SportsCenter* pulling high school jokes while they have a slumber party. Basically, I answer the phone groggily, "Hello?" They say, "Do you have Prince Albert in a Can?" to which I answered several different ways like, "What?" or "Is that you, Kenny?" or "How cheesy!" They had three cameras on me, so the whole scenario took about fifteen minutes to complete.

Mort and I are on a new (earlier) deadline for the book. He's getting married soon, so his days are cluttered with meeting priests, heading up a new website (monsterskate.com), and writing about me—good luck, Sean. I'll try to finish the table of contents before Monday.

A 540 over the hip above the papanazzi in Ocean Beach.

ASEBALL
ONIGHT

"

GeTtInG fRoM
oNe PlAcE tO
aNoThEr At
ThEsE eVeNtS
hAs BeCoMe
VeRy DiFfIcUlT

"

ANOTHER B3 APRIL 17, 2000

Louisville, Kentucky

I went to the event site to check out vert practice and film a segment with Mat Hoffman, the legendary BMX freestyler. We were supposed to reenact a doubles run that we had done a few years ago—this time with a fingerboard and a fingerbike on a Tech Deck halfpipe. Mat asked if we could really ride the ramp, meaning that we would destroy it. Mat landed on it with the back wheels of his bike and it exploded. I ollied onto one of the bigger pieces and flattened it. We continued until it was mere shards of plastic. Kids scrambled for the bits and had us sign each one.

GETTING FROM ONE PLACE TO ANOTHER AT THESE EVENTS HAS BECOME VERY DIFFICULT. Once I leave the fenced-off section of the venue, I get swarmed for autographs. Unless I continue to move as I sign stuff, there is no end in sight. I must come off as rude at some point because it is virtually impossible to fulfill all the requests and actually get anything else done.

The vert event was one of the best I've seen. Bob Burnquist did two incredible runs, adding his repertoire of switch moves like backside ollies and kickflips to fakies. When Bob is on, he is almost impossible to beat. Bucky Lasek also had a great run that tied Bob's first, but he didn't make another one completely so Bob took it. Andy Mac had one of the sketchiest runs I've ever seen, but he threw everything on the wall and stayed on until way past his time was up. He ended up third. It's hard to believe that the skating level keeps improving at each event.

FIT FOR A PRINCE?

MAY 24, 2000

Monte Carlo, Monaco

My sister Pat and I arrived today for the Laureus World Sports Awards, which is an inaugural event awarding excellence in many different sports around the world. I have been nominated in the Alternative Sports category along with Shaun Palmer and Travis Pastrana. Mercedes and Cartier sponsor the whole thing, so no expenses have been spared. As we arrived, the hostess invited us to a lunch cruise on a yacht for all of the invited guests. We would have cut it close by driving, so she offered to arrange a helicopter to take us there. I wasn't really up for another flight, regardless of how short it was, so we got a ride in one of the many Mercedes taxis straight to the hotel.

We went to a party held by *Vogue* in conjunction with the event. Models, including Naomi Campbell and Rebecca Romijn-Stamos, swarmed the pool area in various high-fashion dresses. Boy George was at the turntables and many U.S. television and movie personalities were in attendance. The coolest guy in the place had to be Samuel L. Jackson, so I managed to get a picture with him. Champagne flowed like water. I asked the bartender for a beer and he looked at me like I was an alien. (I already felt like one anyway.) There were two silent auctions for custom concept Mercedes and starting bids were $500,000. I think they both sold. I literally bumped into David Hasselhoff and Sylvester Stallone on the way out. If Mercedes pays, they will come . . .

"the coolest guy in the place had to be Samuel L. Jackson"

MAY 25, 2000

After participating in a regatta this afternoon (on a boat appropriately named *Perseverance*, since it struggled to keep up and barely finished), I went to the hotel, got dressed, and headed to the Awards. Once inside, we were asked to clear the way for another entering guest—Nelson Mandela. Prince Albert of Monaco ("His Serene Highness") was also there.

Shaun walked away with the Best Alternative Athlete award and gave a classy speech about our sports finally gaining some recognition and being treated as equal athletes. In a sports category as broad as "Alternative," Shaun is the obvious choice, since he has dominated more than one. Other winners included Tiger Woods, Marion Jones, Lance Armstrong, and Sergio Garcia. The event lasted three hours, and everyone went to the after party hosted by Cartier. Tables were scarce, and once again we were around a huge crowd of strangers. I felt like I was in the way wherever I stood.

[Left:] The extreme extremists: Shaun Palmer, me, and Travis Pastrana.
[Right:] A bad motherf____ and a skinny dude.

TONY HAWK'S GIGANTIC SKATEPARK TOUR

ESPN ESPN2 EHPN

BY ENTERTAI

Our home away from home: the bus.

GIGANTIC SKATEPARK TOUR JUNE 16, 2000

Home: Carlsbad, California, to Los Angeles, California

The skatepark tour is closing in, so I have been on the phone nonstop tying up loose ends. I've never run into so many difficulties while setting up a tour. One park closed, Bucky got hurt, Brian Anderson is M.I.A., and crossing the Canadian border is going to be too costly with all of the video equipment. On our earlier tours, preproduction mostly involved calling shops and renting a van. It gets more complicated when there are more people and bigger finances involved—at least the missing skaters and canceled parks have been replaced.

I've also been doing a lot of interviews lately regarding the tour. I called our local "alternative" radio station (91X) this morning and talked briefly about our Mission Valley stop with their host. I then drove up to L.A. and did a segment with Pat O'Brien for *Access Hollywood*. His son is an avid skater, so he is a huge supporter of skating endeavors. We talked about the tour, THPS2, and my book. Hopefully it will air before the tour is over. I drove home against L.A. five-o'clock-Friday traffic—bad move. WHEN I GOT HOME, I STARTED PACKING.

JUNE 17, 2000

Home: Carlsbad, California, to Mission Valley: San Diego, California

Everyone flew in to San Diego today to start the tour. Willy Santos, Robert Earl, Frank Barbara, and Morgan Stone came to pick me up in the tour bus—a huge version of a limousine, complete with three satellite TVs and an insane sound system.

The coverage on this tour is going to be very voyeuristic—*Real World* meets *Truth or Dare.* From the moment the bus showed up, there has been a camera on my face recording every movement and conversation. I am slowly learning to deal with the need to make every situation a potential segment for the show. If a decision is to be made, it might be relevant to the programming—so we have to make sure a camera is present. Welcome to *TonyTV.*

When we picked up Andrew Reynolds and Kris Markovich at the airport, you can bet it was a paparazzi scene. All of the tour members went to the hotel and had an orientation meeting. I was surprised at how accepting everyone is to this reality-based approach of covering the tour. Almost all of the skaters agreed to wear wireless microphones while demoing, allowing the viewer to hear exactly what was happening. I don't know how it will turn out, but it will be interesting.

[Left] Did you get that, Trent?
[Right] Kris Monkeyvich at the Playboy Mansion.

240.00

THIS SALE $

141.257

GALLONS

1.699

PRICE PER GALLON $
ALL TAXES INCLUDED

We Welcome

JUNE 18, 2000

Mission Valley: San Diego, California

I woke up for our 9 A.M. production meeting. It was our last-minute preparation for the first demo day. We went to the pool for a training session with Barry Zaritsky, my trainer. He is helping everyone (including me) get over various injuries, and will be with us the entire trip. His techniques are very effective, but militant.

We boarded the bus for our five-minute drive to the park. As we approached, the crowd looked pretty thin. We had to sit on the bus until they had cameras in place to record our grand entrance. We finally got out and started skating street with a few of the locals. Suddenly the park was full of spectators. Willy was ripping the flat bar above the pyramid and Andrew was throwing frontside kickflips with ease. I was having a hard time getting used to my taped-up ankle and dealing with the heat. We skated for nearly an hour, and then I headed over to the vert ramp.

Bob Burnquist and Shaun White joined me on the vert ramp and we had a brief session while trying to fight heat exhaustion. Bob and I did a couple of doubles lines, and then Rick Thorne showed up. Thorne and I tried to do a doubles line and things got ugly. We planned on doing a line where I went over him, we set up twice, and then he would go over me. The first part went well, but when he was supposed to go over me, I could tell (much too late) that he didn't have enough speed. I was already committed to a backside lipslide at that point, so I prepared for the worst. His handlebar jabbed my back, which wasn't too bad, but it sent him flying to the flat bottom. He ended up spraining his wrist and getting a HUGE bruise on his butt cheek. This ended our vert demo.

We took a short break and started our "special event" on the street course. First was a ten-minute jam for a Best Trick event and then we had a Highest Ollie event off of the launch box.

"it was the first of many long days to come"

The judges for the best trick were kids in the audience, so they voted for Shaun White and his melon 360 over the 18-foot launch box. The Highest Ollie event was next—they started the bar at two feet above the launch box and moved it up six inches at a time after everyone had cleared it. If someone missed a height three times, they were out. It started getting gnarly at five feet, and only a few guys made it including Andrew, Kris, Bob, and me. We all managed to clear six feet, so they moved it up to six and a half. I cleared it, but the landing was too sketchy—I had to kick it away. I tried two more times, but I couldn't help thinking about my knee folding during a bad landing. Bob was the only one that managed to make it, so he was declared the winner. He chose to outdo everyone by raising it again and clearing seven feet. He finally gave in at seven and a half. So now if anyone asks Bob how high he can ollie, he can honestly say seven feet (leaving out the jump ramp detail).

WE THEN SIGNED AUTOGRAPHS FOR NEARLY EVERYONE IN ATTENDANCE AND FINALLY LEFT THE PARK FIVE HOURS AFTER WE ARRIVED. THIS WAS LONGER THAN WE HAD PLANNED, BUT THE CROWD SEEMED APPRECIATIVE.

After returning to the hotel, I finally removed the radio microphone from my shirt and exited the camera world to have a Father's Day dinner with Erin and Spencer. It was the first of many long days to come.

[Left.] Rooftop started feeling the vibe coming from the grotto. [Right] Robert Earl is our personal Hef.

"iF tHeSe WaLLS cOULd TaLk"

JUNE 19, 2000

San Diego to Hollywood to Ventura, California

OUR NEXT DESTINATION: THE PLAYBOY MANSION.

Playboy has a group of girls that participate in sports like mountain biking and snowboarding, so they have been donned the clichéd *Playboy* "Extreme Team." They greeted us as we drove up to the mansion and proceeded to give us a tour of the grounds. They showed us Hef's collection of exotic pets, including peacocks and monkeys. We were even invited to swim in the infamous "grotto" pool, to which we didn't hesitate. There is a rock cave in the middle of the pool that houses a giant Jacuzzi and couch-beds around the perimeter. If these walls could talk. As we left, a limo pulled up to the front door and we were quickly escorted out through the back of the compound. Evidently, Hef was about to depart for the NBA Finals (twins in tow) and we were not "cleared" to be in the area. As we slowly made our way to Ventura, we watched the Lakers take the title and their fans take to mindless destruction in their celebration.

PLAYMATES AT PLAY

Caution! Watch for falling silicone.

JUNE 20, 2000
Ventura, California, to Las Vegas, Nevada

As we pulled in to Skate Street, the crowd was lined up around the corner and there was a sizeable audience already inside. We exited the bus and went straight into a street demo. The crowd was pumped and all of the skaters rose to the occasion. *Access Hollywood* was on site covering the event, and they were surprised at the level of excitement in the place. We skated street for nearly an hour, took a break, and did a shorter vert demo. The crowd was lining the deck of the vert ramp, making it difficult to concentrate while waiting for a run. Every ten seconds before I dropped in, kids demanded that I give them my board/pads/helmet/watch/shoes/kidneys/soul, and I briefly escaped their grasp. I finally quit skating due more to mental than physical exhaustion.

WE TOOK ANOTHER BREAK AND HELD THE BEST TRICK EVENT ON ONE OF THE FUN BOXES ON THE COURSE.

Danny Way showed up late, but managed to pull a 360 flip to frontside 50/50 all the way across. Billy-Joe, one of the locals, made a perfect kickflip noseslide during the 10-minute jam. In the end, Andrew won it with a frontside kickflip up and over the ledge to the flat. I was merely a spectator in the whole thing. We all went outside for a lengthy autograph session and got on the bus headed straight to Vegas.

Many detours and missed turns later, we pulled up to the Hard Rock Hotel at 2 A.M. Our sleeping patterns are anything but normal with this schedule, so we all headed to the casino. A couple hours later, Andrew was up $1,000 from a streak of roulette winnings. I went to bed with a little more than I started with. We are here for two more nights, so things could get ugly. . . .

JUNE 22, 2000

After a pool session with Barry, I got dressed, taped up, and got on the bus headed to the demo. As we drove up, we could tell that the crowd wasn't going to be a problem. This venue got changed four days ago, so we were concerned that people wouldn't get the message. I guess the radio interview we did yesterday helped. The street course was very small, but it had enough elements to make things interesting. Andrew kickflipped off the top of the launch box straight to flat, and Ellis did a pivot-to-fakie on the huge vert wall. Rooftop almost killed himself on a blunt to fakie on a shaky fence way above a quarterpipe, and finally landed it in the end. We took a break and went to the vert ramp. It was the smallest vert ramp I've skated in a while, with more flat bottom than any other. Needless to say, it took a while to get used to. Thorne and I did some doubles, this time without incident. Ellis tried to bomb-drop from an eight-foot-high platform. He tried it over and over, slamming onto his elbow and hip until he finally gave up. By the end, a collective wager was up to $600 for a make. We gave him part of it just for the effort and abuse. This park wasn't suitable for a Best Trick event, so we went straight into lengthy autograph session.

We all ended up in the casino where our invincible winning attitudes were shattered. By the end of the night, I lost everything I had won, and Andrew had three dollars to his name. There is a reason they give out free drinks while you sit at a casino gambling table: It impairs your judgment.

JUNE 24, 2000
Las Vegas, Nevada, to Salt Lake City, Utah

I finally slept in for once. We spent most of the day in the hotel doing wrap-up interviews for the first week of the tour. We left at 5:30 P.M. for our scheduled demo at Real Ride Skatepark. The crowd was huge as we walked in, and the street demo was exciting. Willy Santos flew in yesterday. He and I had a double-flip retro session during which I landed a double 360 flip for the first time in seven years. Andrew and Kris went through an encyclopedia of flip tricks over the course of an hour.

I took a break and went over to the vert ramp. I've been sick since the start of the trip, and it's been taking its toll on my body. I struggled to stay on tricks that I could practically do in my sleep. I finally gave up after landing a 720 and went back to the bus, wheezing and hacking worse than ever. We did an autograph session and finally left the park at 10:30 P.M. We came back to the hotel, cleaned up the bus, and got packed OUR FLIGHTS LEAVE EARLY, AND I CAN'T WAIT TO GET HOME FOR A FEW DAYS.

THE EAST COAST LEG

JULY 8, 2000

Jacksonville, Florida

I woke up at 8:30 A.M. and had breakfast with our new crew—Danny Way, Brian Sumner, Alex Chalmers, Jason Ellis, Robert Earl, Sal Masakela, Rooftop, Bam Margera, and Anthony Furlong.

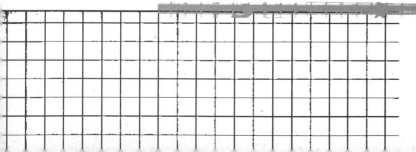

Six hundred ninety-six thousand, nine-hundred and sixty-nine.

The crowd at Kona Skatepark could only be compared to one at a rock concert. They had presold 3,000 tickets and estimated that at least another 1,000 people showed up. Wading through the mob toward the street course was a challenge; autograph requests were literally shoved in front of my face while I was simply trying to keep track of Riley's whereabouts. We skated the street course for about forty–five minutes. Brian nailed the hardest tricks over the pyramid and Ellis did a backside nosegrind on the biggest extension. I was stoked on doing a crooked grind down the main handrail and not rolling my ankle again. Alex was trying to do a kickflip Indy 360 over the launch box as we neared the end. He finally tried to stick one and ended up folding his foot so that his toes touched the top of his ankle. This marked the end of our street session and the beginning of his rehabilitation.

We took a long break in the bus and the "vert jocks" (myself included) got to work. Jason, Anthony, Danny, and I joined the numerous locals for at least an hour-long vert demo. Danny had an idea for doubles where we would do McTwists on the same wall and then he would do a frontside 540 (Rodeo) underneath my frontside air. It seemed to work as planned, and it got a huge crowd response. I learned later that we were inches away from each other as we crossed, barely making it safely. I could tell that he was close, but I didn't think it was such a near miss. A collision would have sent us both to our backs.

Bottom view of an overturn grind. You never realize the effort that goes into a photo like this (mostly from the photographer). In this case, Grant nailed some wood on the ramp and risked a broken nose/camera to get close.

"there has been an ongoing dare with Sal to drop in on a vert ramp, and it seemed that this was the day"

There has been an ongoing dare with Sal to drop in on a vert ramp, and it seemed that this was the day. A collective $420 was raised for the bet, and Sal rose to the occasion. His first few attempts were hopeless (he wasn't really trying), so he went and warmed up on the miniramp. When he returned, he had the fire in his eyes. He started making it to the flat bottom using my board, but finally decided that my trucks were too loose. I keep my trucks tight, but I forgot about the approximate fifty-pound weight difference when I offered it to him. He finally got the hang of it on Danny's board and made one perfectly to a supportive crowd. The rest of the crew flanked him on the flat bottom and Sal left with a permasmile.

JULY 9, 2000

I woke up to a door knock somewhere around 9 A.M. Upon answering it, I found Bam, Morgan, Matty, and Rob waiting to get in. Bam wanted to jump from the top story of the hotel into the pool, and my room—on the 6th floor—was in the perfect place. I wiped the sleep from my eyes and set up my digital camera just in time to witness the stunt. Bam climbed onto our railing while yelling at Barry (who was in the shallow end of the pool) to "Ice this!" and jumped down to the 8.5-foot deep end. He landed and barely got his head underwater before emerging victorious. Erin stayed in the room the entire time, refusing to watch and worrying for his safety. Riley thought it was cool and mused about doing it himself. Yeah, right.

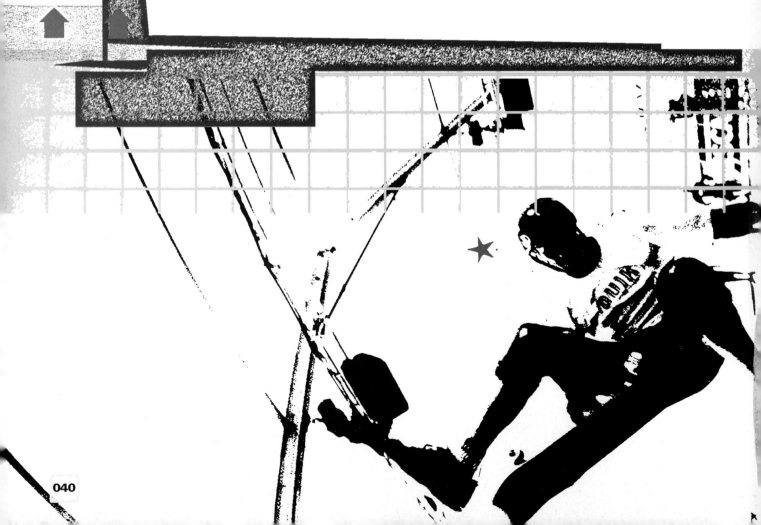

Bam's jump. I couldn't get the water in the frame, so it looks like a suicide attempt instead of a high dive.

Varial 540: Skate Street, Ventura, CA.

JULY 10, 2000
Atlanta, Georgia

We got our stuff together after breakfast and headed to our demo at the Extreme Sports Park in Duluth.

The place was not too crowded, which was actually a relief after all of these overwhelming turnouts. We found out later that they could only let four hundred people in due to fire codes and turned away anyone else that showed up. The street demo went very well, and the highlights included Brian doing frontside bluntslides and a kickflip to five-0 on the handrail. Riley did a backside 180 off a five-foot deck. As we were winding down, Danny tried a 360 method over the launch box, bailed, and badly twisted his knee. He took a break and realized that the damage was severe enough to get an operation. Brian's wife was also scheduled for surgery the following day due to pregnancy complications, so he and Danny caught flights home.

Anthony, Jason, and I did a vert demo that seemed to go well, but was a little rough with so few people skating.

JULY 11, 2000
Atlanta, Georgia, to Winston-Salem/Wilmington, NC

After another night of less than four hours of sleep, I caught my flight to North Carolina. Barry had arranged a number of tests at a hospital in High Point, North Carolina (near Winston-Salem) to figure out my exact breathing ailment. We had a tight schedule and in a matter of seven hours, I had undergone X rays, an MRI, breathing tests, allergy tests, and blood tests. The verdict was enlightening: I have a number of allergies that I never knew about including grass, mold, mildew, and rug mites.

Barry and I flew to Wilmington and arrived at 11 P.M., almost the same time as the tour bus, which was also carrying my family. We went to sleep somewhere around 1 A.M., only to be woken up by a screaming Sal in the hallway an hour later. Apparently Rooftop and Bam had dismantled his bed, putting his box springs in the bathroom, his mattress over the window, and all of his towels in the toilet. It was another sporadic night of sleep.

JULY 13, 2000
Richmond, Virginia, to Hartford, Connecticut, to Providence, Rhode Island

I spent all day riding on the bus and catching up on journal entries. I even got a little more sleep. At any given time, there is a crew watching a DVD, others playing THPS2, some sleeping, and a heated game of blackjack at the main table. This particular blackjack marathon went on for nearly eight hours with Trent acting as the casino/house/bank. This would normally be to his advantage, but we (peer pressure is rough) took him to the cleaners. At one point, Trent was out over $2,500, with most of it going to Rob, Sal, and myself. We started betting bigger hands out of guilt, assuming we would lose and still won. By the end, he was still down, but not by too much. We broke the bank.

We were then handed passes to a Foo Fighters/Red Hot Chili Peppers concert and led backstage so that we could watch from the side. The Foo Fighters were great, and we mingled a bit after their show. They said that THPS is a major activity on their bus while on this tour.

"everyone decided that i was their target of destruction"

I guess the whole rock star thing got into our crew's blood. As we drove to Providence, DMX was blasting in the back room and it suddenly turned into a wrestling match/music video. Everyone crowded around a camera and did their best gangsta imitations, which evolved into a giant pile-up with at least ten guys bouncing off the walls and each other. For some reason, the tide turned and everyone decided that I was their target of destruction. They grabbed all available shoelaces and attempted to hog-tie me for who knows what purpose. I managed to keep my hands free most of the time and caught a glimpse of my saving grace amidst the chaos: a bottle of Cheez Whiz wedged into the seat. Without anyone seeing, I squirted a handful and splattered it across the faces of my culprits. They were stunned, and I managed to hop away. I didn't get very far—they caught me and covered me in my own weapon. At least it was closure to my abuse. I have to thank Kris for trying to save me from complete destruction. Trent walked away with a bloody lip, and we all left the bus at 3 A.M. smelling like a nacho cheese factory.

This ramp was custom built for a Bagel Bites commercial in downtown Los Angeles; backside nosegrind across the twelve-foot "bridge of death."

Tanned and feathered . . . I mean, cheesed and taped.

JULY 14, 2000
Middletown, Rhode Island

At Skater's Island, I did a few newspaper interviews and got padded up for the vert demo. Bucky was throwing rodeo flips over the channel and every heelflip possible. There was a rumor going around that Richard Lopez, a local vert pro, had recently landed a 900. He joined in, and there was an ongoing buzz from the locals that he would try it. As we winded down, he went for one. He had the fastest spin I've seen, like that of a gymnast. He spins more straight up and down, which I think makes it harder to compensate for a sketchy landing and forces him to spin more. After about five tries, I offered him $500 to make one. This started a 900 fund that just kept growing. Ron Semaio, ESPN's programming director, threw in $1,000, and almost every other skater from our tour pitched in. By the time he was getting close, the total was somewhere around $3,300. He took a big slam after a wobbly take off and just kept trying. He landed a couple on the wall, but was leaning a little too far forward to compensate for the flat bottom. After a valiant effort, his time was up. I be-lieve that he has made it after seeing his technique and perseverance. The ramp was too small for me to try it, but I wouldn't have anyway. It was his moment, and I was stoked just to watch. ESPN gave him half of the money just for trying. The crowd loved it.

The East Coast leg is over and it was a huge success. I will be home for two days before heading to Japan. The notion of sleep consumes me.

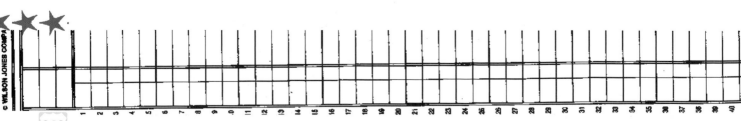

Riley, backside 180 in Tokyo.

"BaM Took a dETour by ThE high divEs"

Bam scores a perfect ten for insanity.

SUSHI TOUR JULY 20, 2000

Tokyo, Japan

We arrived last night for a whirlwind Adio/Hawk Shoes tour. The crew consists of Bam Margera, Ed Selego, Danny Montoya, Jeff Taylor, Jared Prindle, Riley, and myself. We all passed out after arriving at our hotel last night somewhere around 7 P.M. Everyone was awake by 5 A.M. and ready to go into a city that was utterly closed. Some guys went skating around our hotel, but only managed to find rough sidewalks and streets. The stairs, rails, and ledges had potential, but the riding surface was always a problem. We finally left the hotel around 10 A.M. and headed to our first demo.

After a drive that was originally estimated at an hour but turned into three (as is the case with driving anywhere in Tokyo), we arrived at the Oisin hotel/resort right on the beach. It was a compound of swimming pools, water slides, high dives, and even a small FlowRider wave pool. There was already a street course and "vert" ramp set up in the parking lot. We did two short street demos where the MC would introduce us one by one, have us do a couple of tricks, and move on to the next guy. We were finished before we knew it. It was way too hot for any of us to complain about not skating enough, so we didn't say much about the obscure format. I moved on to the vert ramp, which was no more than nine and a half feet high and only twelve feet wide (some would consider it a miniramp). Bam put it best when he said, "even quarterpipes are wider than twelve feet these days!" I skated for about fifteen minutes and they decided that it was enough. Everything in our schedule here seems rushed, but that seems to be the way they want it.

After our "demos," we were on our way to the FlowRider when Bam took a detour by the high dives and decided to ollie off the top. It was one of the scariest stunts I've seen, and I can't believe that he kept the board under his feet until impact. The lifeguard was befuddled (and pissed off), but luckily I got the shot. We then went over to the FlowRider for a free-for-all session that resembled another demo more than anything, judging by the crowd.

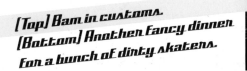

[Top] Bam in customs.
[Bottom] Another fancy dinner
for a bunch of dirty skaters.

JULY 21, 2000

Woke up at 3:30 A.M. to my bed shaking violently. I first thought that Riley had risen too early and was trying to get me up as well. When I noticed that he was still asleep, I figured that I was on course for an exorcism. I finally realized that it was an earthquake and that we were on the twenty-sixth floor of the Keio Plaza hotel. Growing up in California, you get used to the occasional tremor but this was more than I've usually experienced. We found out later that it measured 6.7 on the Richter and did absolutely no damage to Tokyo—they aren't kidding around about building codes here.

Riley: Have a skateboard, will travel.

Riley feeling like a Japanese superhero.

hOpEfUlLy NeXt TiMe ThEy WiLl AlL uNdErStAnD tHe ImPoRtAnCe Of CaTeRiNg To ThE hArDcOrE sKaTeRs

JULY 23, 2000

Woke up way too early (again). We left the hotel at noon and drove for two hours to do a demo at a Japanese skate competition. At last . . . we were in our element and skating for skaters. There were about two hundred entrants and two thousand people watching. Because of the unexpected number of participants, we waited for our turn to skate. When it finally came, we were only allowed to session for twenty minutes—just enough time to get warmed up. I was in the middle of trying rodeo flips over a spine ramp when the announcer said something about ending our demo. The crowd immediately rushed the course, making it completely unskateable. I guess we were finished at that point. They announced the winners of the competition while we signed autographs.

As the awards presentation finished, they tried to pull me away from signing stuff so that we could leave. I was frustrated—I couldn't figure out why we came all the way to Japan to skate a couple of brief demos and not sign autographs or make ourselves available to the local skaters. I managed to ignore the constant requests to leave just long enough to appease immediate autograph and picture requests. We later learned that there was a miscommunication between the competition organizers and our distributor, leading to our hurried exhibition. Hopefully next time they will all understand the importance of catering to the hardcore skaters—the ones who will keep the Japanese skate scene alive in the future.

Signing as seen on the big monitors.

SLP

"tHiS iS OnE oF tHe CrAzIeSt ScHeDuLeS i'Ve EvEr FoLLoWeD iN tErMs oF NoNsToP cOmMitMeNts"

THE BOOK TOUR AUGUST 6, 2000

New York City

I got in to New York City a little past midnight. I then had to wake up early this morning to do a newspaper interview. I had lunch with a few members of the publishing staff from ReganBooks, and headed over to the Virgin Megastore in Times Square for the signing. The security was tight and too overbearing at times. I was a little surprised that the crowd was smaller than yesterday's crowd at Borders bookstore in Chicago, but privately relieved. This is one of the craziest schedules I've ever followed in terms of nonstop commitments. My first commitment tomorrow begins at 8 A.M. and doesn't stop until I board a flight for Houston later that night.

The view from TRL.

Signing away in Times Square.

I hate it when Sean does that.

TOUR SCHEDULE (DAY 3)
HERE WAS MY PROPOSED SCHEDULE FOR AUGUST 7, 2000:

9:45 A.M.	*Arrival*	**MTV Radio (CBS Studios)**
10:00 A.M. to 11:00 A.M.		**Radio satellite**
11:30 A.M.	*Arrival*	**CBS-TV**
11:45 A.M. to 1:00 P.M.	*Meeting*	**Late Show with David Letterman**
		Meeting with producer to discuss plans for Tony's Letterman appearance on August 30.
1:30 P.M.	*Arrival*	**NEW YORK TIMES**
1:45 P.M. to 2:45 P.M.	*Interview*	Interview will be at the Omni Berkshire Place restaurant in the atrium. Interview will also include a photographer. Story will appear in the sports section. Run date to come.
2:50 P.M.	*Arrival*	**PLATFORM NETWORK**
3:00 P.M. to 4:00 P.M.	*Interview*	Interview will be at the Omni Hotel restaurant in the atrium and will include video for on-line streaming.
4:30 P.M.	*Arrival*	**METRO CHANNEL**
5:00 P.M. to 6:00 P.M.	*Live Interview*	Studio Y
7:45 P.M.	*Leave NYC/ La Guardia*	**Continental Flight 1963**
10:37 P.M.	*Arrive Houston*	**Houston Intercontinental**

Everything basically went as planned . . . there were a few minor details left out—such as finding time to eat, designing a mini-skatepark to be built on David Letterman's studio roof, helping to edit our next ESPN Gigantic Skatepark Tour show (due to ESPN tomorrow and airing on Tuesday), a few conference calls via cell phone, a bitchy newspaper photographer, and a three-hour flight delay that put me into Houston at 2 A.M. Sleep, what sleep?

THE 2000 SUMMER
X GAMES AUGUST 16, 2000

San Francisco, California

Erin, Spencer, and I were scheduled to fly here this morning so I could conduct an interview with the *Wall Street Journal* at our hotel before my book signing at 2:30 P.M. Our flight was two hours late thanks to United's recent business woes, and I had to do the interview hurriedly in the car on the way to the bookstore. THE SIGNING WENT WELL—IT WAS SCHEDULED FOR TWO HOURS AND I MANAGED TO GET TO THE END OF THE LINE IN THAT TIME WITHOUT RUSHING ANYONE.

"my ankle survived but my wrist went numb"

From there I went to shoot a segment for ESPN about real street skating in San Francisco. Chris Senn, Kyle Berard, and Dayne Brummet joined us as we went to a huge ledge in Chinatown and then to the China Banks. I haven't been to the China Banks since shooting *Animal Chin* in 1986, so I attempted to skate even though my ankle was swollen from practicing doubles with Andy yesterday. After trying to clear one of the benches going frontside, I came down the wall and stopped as my nose dug into the flat, sending me sprawling across the bricks. My ankle survived, but my wrist went numb. I did interviews with the skaters from that point on, asking them what the main difference is between this style of skating and competitive "street" skating (aka "park" skating). Needless to say, there weren't any philosophical revelations in our conversations. The bottom line: you don't find perfect vertical quarterpipes and perfectly shaped ledges out in the street. We stayed at the banks until dark and missed an integral part of real street skating: getting kicked out of a spot.

A 360 Flip to Fakie, Gigantic Skatepark Tour, Charlotte, NC, 2002.

AUGUST 17, 2000

I woke up to the Spencer alarm clock this morning. I went to the X Games kickoff show where they presented me with an "It doesn't get any better" award. The girl from *American Beauty* (Mena Suvari) presented it to me by reading the cue card as if she were being forced to do so. The crowd started chanting her monologue (since they were in view of the cards) just to get things moving along. I accepted the award and got congratulations from Andy Dick. Then No Doubt played a couple of songs.

I went over to the vert ramp and snaked into the practice session partly to get a feel for the ramp and partly because I couldn't stay away. I then took off my pads and did some brief interviews with the skaters. Bucky placed first in the prelims while skating to our tour anthem—"Party Up" by DMX.

Varial heelflip melon to fakie across the channel in Zurich—got that?

AUGUST 18, 2000

The vert finals were amazing to watch—Bucky was in the lead the entire time until Pierre-Luc Gagnon nailed a run that put him in first. It was all down to Bucky's final run—the last one of the entire event. He made everything he tried, including a frontside heelflip gay twist (that he never made in practice). Colin McKay also ripped and placed third. I ran around doing interviews behind the scenes after each run while trying in vain to watch everyone else's performance.

We left and headed to a radio station where a few of us had semipermission to briefly take over the programming courtesy of Robert Earl. As we (Rob, Jason Ellis, Bucky, Rick Thorne, and Sal Masakela) entered the studio, the working DJ (Noname) was naked. We literally took over the airwaves by tying Noname to his chair and playing whatever we wanted (DMX, the Clash, and the Faction) uncensored. We would cut off some of the songs halfway through to scream nonsense and answer some of the many calls that were coming in. Since Noname was tied up, we couldn't figure out how

Our biggest turnout to date: Gigantic Skatepark Tour, Louisville, KY, 2002.

to get the phone conversations into the broadcast. We ended up talking to the callers, but anyone listening could only hear our voices instead of a two-way conversation. I guess we should have planned better.

Spencer and Riley give the sports update, Atlanta, GA.

AUGUST 19, 2000

When I woke up I headed straight to the vert ramp for doubles practice. Andy and I worked on our routines and ended up changing one right before the event started, which got us both confused. We decided to stay with the original plan at the last minute and placed first in the preliminaries. As the finals neared, the wind kicked in and made some of our combos nearly impossible.

Sean Penn was spotted in the stands, so Andy and I introduced ourselves. We wanted to let him know that there is a trick named after him (backside Madonna = Sean Penn), and he was very cool. I was tempted to throw some Spicoli lines at him, but I'm sure he's heard them all (just like when I get *Animal Chin* quotes randomly yelled at me).

Andy and I made our first run, and I was stoked that I didn't screw up while holding my board out as he did a frontside pivot on it (like I did a few times in practice). **OUR SECOND RUN GOT OFF TO A BAD START AS ANDY BOTTOM–LANDED HIS FIRST SETUP AIR AND BAILED A VARIAL 540.** We started over and made it to the end of the run, but I had the same problem setting up for a 720, so our finale didn't come together. I was hoping we would make it to the end so that I could do a five-0 board transfer that we had worked on, but the wind got the better of us. In any case, it was a fun event—I like seeing what new things we can come up with each time.

I rushed out in order to make it to Erin's ten-year high school reunion in Santa Rosa. The drive took forever, thanks to ridiculous San Francisco traffic. I didn't go to my own reunion, since I knew practically nobody in my class. I knew even fewer at this one so fellow husbands TJ, Jason, and I lurked in the background the whole time. I forgot that the popular music from 1990 was so bad . . .

AUGUST 20, 2000

I drove back to San Francisco to tape another show segment about the vert finals and skate during the Best Trick practice. I could see Bob trying a few crazy things, but waiting until the contest started in order to really try to make them. **THE CONTEST GOT OFF TO A SLOW START AS EVERYBODY TRIED THEIR HARDEST STUFF.** Andy made a few nollie heelflip variations and Tas Pappas made a kickflip varial Indy 360. He then tried to spin some 9s, but the wind was once again in effect. Bob turned the bench obstacle upright and made a rock to fakie on the makeshift eight-foot vertical extension. Andy made a lien to tail on it as well. As the contest wound down, Colin made a nollie kickflip backside tailslide revert. Bob dropped in next and made a fakie ollie to fakie frontside five-0 to kickflip on the raised bar above the coping. He had been trying it sporadically throughout the event and it was questionable whether he would make it. His board bounced off the bottom coping as it was still flipping and he was the most surprised out of anyone that he actually rode away. As if that wasn't enough, he started trying alley-oop backside tailslide reverts as the time ran out. It was an incredible event to watch, and I went back to the hotel fired up about learning new stuff.

We got a ride back with Danny DeVito and his son, and they couldn't stop raving about the event. He even invited us to dinner, but we had already made plans. It is amazing to see so many celebrities make the effort to experience the X Games, which was considered a goofy sideshow at its inception.

I'm here until the twenty-second, doing Bagel Bites and book promotion, then (thankfully) I get to go home on the twenty-third.

Stalefish 540, Mall of America.

THPS2 SHOWDOWN

SEPTEMBER 16, 2000
Boardrider's Club: Seattle, Washington

Flew in this morning for a Quiksilver promotion and grand opening of their Boardrider's Club (Quiksilver retail store). After checking into our hotel, we headed straight to a new skatepark placed right under the famed Space Needle. Then we went to the Boardrider's Club, where one hundred winners got a chance to come in and hang out, get autographs, play THPS2, and discuss quantum mechanics theory. One kid kept hounding me to play against him in a one-on-one game of THPS2, claiming that he would "take me out." I tried to avoid the challenge, mainly because we were still signing stuff, but also because I know how much time kids devote to playing the game (and I don't get nearly as much practice). I went over to show some of the employees a few secret areas and codes (nothing supersecret). The kid that was to take me out somehow materialized during my game, so I was stuck. He grabbed the other controller and we had a showdown. He talked the talk, but didn't walk the walk. He left the store after two games mumbling something about "next time . . ."

Tight trannie + long legs × Frontside rock = don't bail.

Good luck finding a place to lie down if you're late boarding the bus.

"my gEnerAL sleePinG paTTern whIlE in EurOpE iS a seRieS Of tWo- to fOUr-hour NaPs streWn in bEtweeN oBliGatioNs and fEsTiViTes. I GueSS it woRkS, foR A liTTle wHile"

SWISS ACCOUNT

SEPTEMBER 23, 2000

Freestyle.ch: Zurich, Germany

I arrived in Zurich at 10 A.M. after a three-hour delay in Dallas, Texas. This is my fifth year in a row doing the Freestyle.ch, a huge event that includes a snowboard big-air event, BMX, freestyle motocross, a street course, and a huge vert.

They decided to have a formal vert contest this year, as opposed to the jam sessions we have had in the past. I was only scheduled to skate during the last day of the event, but I flew in a day earlier in order to shoot some photos for the Quiksilver Europe crew. They had Afiff Bellakdar—one of the best skate photographers in Europe—fly in from Paris for the day to take the pictures.

We had a scheduled time on the ramp for this particular shoot, and they didn't let any other photographers on the ramp. Some people were miffed at that request, but we just didn't want to have a good photo ruined by someone else's camera in the foreground. It was strange to be doing this sort of thing in front of a crowd—usually photo shoots are more low-key since you're trying one thing at a time and not doing full runs. They also consist of a lot of bails when you're trying something hard. In any case, we managed to get some good sequences (alley-oop five over the channel, Indy 7, heelflip varial melon to fakie over the channel, and various air shots).

Affif, Jared, Jasper (a Quicksilver Europe rep), and I left there and headed to the annual Freestyle.ch party, a warehouse-style club/rave with three separate rooms with different styles of music (techno, hip-hop, and another that could only be described as drug-induced). Once we got in the car, I fell asleep for nearly two hours while Jasper and crew got lost over and over trying to find the place.

> "i arose to the dreaded wake-up call, gathered my composure, and went to the event site"

We finally got there and we all stayed way too late, mostly hanging out in the hip-hop room and the VIP area, where free food and drinks were hard to resist. Went back to the hotel as the sun was creeping up. I realized that I had to skate in less than six hours—smooth move. My general sleeping pattern while in Europe is a series of two- to four-hour naps strewn in between obligations and festivities. I guess it works, for a little while.

SEPTEMBER 24, 2000

I arose to the dreaded wake-up call, gathered my composure, and went to the event site. From there, I was pulled nonstop from interview to autograph session to skate demo to interview and over again.

During the last demo, which consisted of Sandro Dias, Sasha Steinhorst, and myself, I was finally getting burned out. Sandro pulled a *huge* alley-oop melon five over the channel, and it got me fired up. If there was ever a portable ramp ideal for spinning 9s, this was it. I tested a couple and they felt consistent. As long as I landed two good setup airs, the spin wasn't a problem. I tested it a few more times and started to commit to the landing. I shot out on one and landed right on my ass, burning a hole in my shorts and bestowing myself with nice hipper. The crowd was incredibly supportive, cheering louder every time I climbed the ladder to try again. I finally stuck one (albeit with a signature squat) and it felt great to finally make it again. After slamming at Encinitas and Woodward the last two times I tried it, my confidence level was suffering—I started to feel like I was destined to get hurt on 9s from now on.

I don't speak German, so this is probably not as in-depth an interview as it appears to be.

Indy gay twist, Chelsea Piers, NYC, prior to 9/11.

A 9 WHEN YOU LEAST EXPECT IT OCTOBER 1, 2000

Rock-n-Air Festival: Denver, Colorado

Flew in from Vegas this morning after Mort's bachelor party and roughly two hours of sleep. The Red Bull Rock-n-Air event was a festival that included bands, snowboarding, and the Red Bull ramp (for skaters and BMXers) held at the famous Red Rock Amphitheater. Kid Rock was sitting in front of us on the plane ride, and I assumed he was going to the same event, since Pennywise (who were slated to perform) were also on our plane. Upon our asking, he knew nothing about the event but told us he was going to a wedding. It must be the season—Mort's wedding is next weekend and Kris Markovich's is the one after.

Kris Markovich, aka Spiderman of street.

We checked in to the hotel, grabbed some sandwiches, and went straight to the event. Our first demo was scheduled for two hours, which was optimistic at best. I met up with Sergie Ventura, Phil Hajal, Mat Hoffman, Rick Thorne, and Jamie Bestwick, and we all started riding. The Red Bull ramp is excellent as far as portable ramps go. We all burned out about an hour into our demo. I wanted to try a 9, since the ramp was set up at full width and there would be plenty of room. One wall was slightly over-vert, which actually worked to my advantage for getting around. I tried one, completely missed my board, but luckily came around without any major mishap. I tried a few more and they felt good. I finally set one down and shot out on the flat bottom—but I came out standing up instead of squatting on my board. This was a first and I was stoked even though I slammed on the flat. I ran back up and did the exact same thing—and it worked. I popped up on the other side in disbelief, expecting to fall backward at some point before I got there. I always hoped to land one properly and am thankful that Red Bull has the foresight to make such a big demo ramp for us to enjoy.

Mat Hoffman, Vagabond Inn, Fresno, CA.

Lien air, Southside Statepark,
Houston, FL.

SCRAMBLE NOVEMBER 4, 2000

Home to Dallas, Texas, to Houston, Texas

Woke up at 5:30 A.M. in order to catch my 6:50 A.M. flight. Chris Miller and I were headed to Dallas for a quick store appearance before flying to Houston for the annual Make-A-Wish benefit. Our flight to Los Angeles was delayed (United strikes again), and we got there just after our Dallas flight took off. This put us three hours behind schedule and made us an hour and a half late for the shop signing. We could see the line all the way out of the mall as we approached. **I SAT DOWN AND SIGNED AUTOGRAPHS FOR FOUR HOURS STRAIGHT.**

I wonder if people who wait in autograph lines actually believe that we are delayed by no fault of our own, or if they think that we are careless and lackadaisical with these types of commitments—and late because we just don't care that much. I imagine that they picture us lounging poolside, umbrella drinks in hand, muttering "They can wait a little more." In my defense, I can honestly say that I always get to the airport on time to make my scheduled departure. What happens from there is usually out of my hands. It's funny when people throw guilt-trip lines at you like "We've been waiting here for three hours." If they only knew when my journey began just to be there . . .

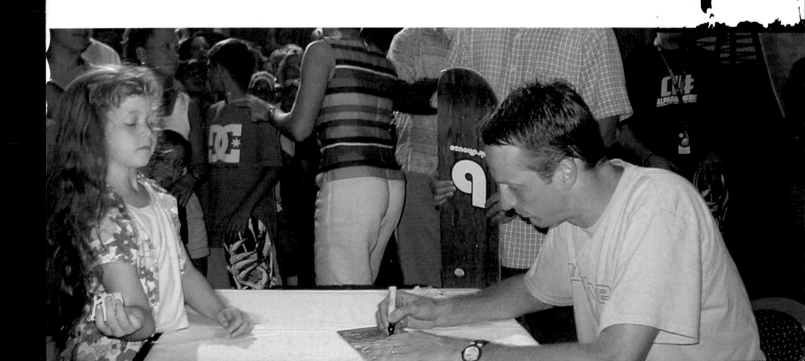

THE NEW GUY

NOVEMBER 7, 2000

Election Day: Austin, Texas

I arrived last night for a day of filming for a new movie titled *The New Guy*. It's a high school comedy with adult-type humor. I am doing a cameo in a house party scene where I skate a miniramp in the front yard. We were scheduled to shoot outside all night, but the rain put everything on hold.

A few of the cast members and I went out in downtown Austin to see the election mayhem, since George W. Bush was scheduled to give a victory/consolation speech. The restaurants and bars were packed with people glued to TVs. They would cheer as Bush would win a state's electoral vote and cower as Gore kept up in the race. I didn't vote . . . not because of a disinterest, but because I got called to this movie at the last minute and didn't have time to mail in my ballot. I was down for Gore (or Nader), but that is not something you want to make public while in Austin during election night, especially with a bunch of drunk Republicans who aren't sure whether to open the Champagne or start brawling.

NOVEMBER 8, 2000

I got picked up at 4 P.M. and driven to the set, where it was seriously cold and only getting colder. The "ramp" they had set up for me was a joke, since nobody in production consulted skaters (or me) when building it. They had two quarterpipes four feet high, four feet wide, with four-foot transitions, and a four-foot vert ramp that wasn't wide enough (or strong enough) to do anything. I got them to build two more at the last minute that were stronger and had bigger trannies. I couldn't do much except blunts and disasters.

They had a wedge ramp set up to the back of one of the quarterpipes for a motorcycle stunt. This formed a makeshift launch box, which I rode by being towed by a motorcycle since the street was too rough to push into it. The director seemed happy with this, so I did a few jumps for the cameras and tried a few 360s at the end. It was too hard to judge the speed from the motorcycle, and I ended up bailing five or six before setting one down and falling on the flat. If they do use any of the 360 shots in the movie, I don't claim to have made one. I finished another scene where they shot my reaction to the moto jump and then I was out at 2 A.M.

Indy 360 over the 40-foot gap at "Bart's Extreme Extravaganza."

ONE MORE HAWK

NOVEMBER 9, 2000

Austin, Texas, to Los Angeles, California, to San Diego, California

I caught my flight in a sleepless daze and slept all the way to Los Angeles. Got picked up by a Town Car and driven to Fox Studios to shoot *Turn Ben Stein On*—a new talk show starring the host of *Win Ben Stein's Money* . . . Ben Stein.

I finished there and headed straight home just in time to get dressed and go to the San Diego Hall of Champions, where they put up a display of my pictures and memorabilia that will be exhibited through February. It is the first time they have recognized any "nontraditional" sport in their museum, and it was the best response they have ever had in terms of turnout. I was honored to have been chosen to represent skateboarding, and I have a feeling it will not be the first time they highlight a skater in their exhibits.

To add to today's craziness, we found out (during my one hour at home) that Erin is pregnant. We are all very excited.

Always on camera; no time to be sick on tour.

WILLY'S MAYHEM

DECEMBER 3, 2000

Willy's Workshop: San Diego, California

I agreed to do an autograph session at Willy's new shop to help him get things rolling. It was scheduled to be from noon to 2 P.M.

Erin has been bedridden with morning sickness since Thanksgiving, and luckily I have been around to help her. With this in mind, I had to make sure that this signing ran smoothly and didn't turn into a four- to five-hour ordeal. I asked the staff to assign someone to stand at the end of the line, so that as our time came to an end they could kindly tell people who weren't already waiting that the line had been cut off. Doing it this way allows the people who have already been standing in line the chance to get their autographs, and late comers don't wait in line only to get rejected when the time is up.

At 2:30 P.M. there was no end in sight, and whoever was supposed to be the end-of-liner didn't stick around to follow through with his task. Normally I can stay and try to push through, but Erin was home with severe nausea while trying to look after two-year-old Spencer by herself. The shop cut the line off at the front and people were not happy. I felt terrible about the situation, but I really didn't have a choice in the matter. Knowing how many kids waited for nothing made me almost as nauseous as my wife . . .

BILLBOARD (HEAD) BASH

DECEMBER 5, 2000

Billboard Music Awards: Las Vegas, Nevada

I was invited to be an award presenter at the *Billboard* Music Awards. The producers allowed me to take four guests along for the trip, and provided them with an extra room and passes to every event. The 900 Films crew—Morgan and Matty—joined me. I left yesterday, but Erin was not sure about making it on a plane (or leaving the house, for that matter). She said she would make every effort to fly out the day of the awards (today).

THIS MORNING I WENT TO THE *BILLBOARD* AWARDS REHEARSAL WHILE EVERYONE SLEPT IN. They asked us to be there by 10 A.M. to run through the entire event. As I walked in, *NSync was rehearsing a dance routine. There were cardboard cutouts of select presenters and performers in empty seats so that the cameras would know exactly where to find Britney Spears or Oscar De La Hoya if they needed a close-up. I waited while bands like Vertical Horizon and BBMak mingled in the aisles waiting for their turn onstage. After an hour and a half they called me to the stage to rehearse with Pink. I did not know who Pink was until I got here, but I learned that she was a hardcore skater and had even been to Woodward skate camp three summers in a row. She was very nice and we waited almost another half hour by the side of the stage while Destiny's Child kept restarting their number. The stage producer finally said that we didn't need to wait any longer as long as we were comfortable with our lines and positions at the podium. We left without hesitation.

As I was leaving, a woman handed me an invitation to "The Lounge," which was a room full of mini-kiosks with different product manufacturers and distributors at each one. It was basically a fancy goody bag for the performers and presenters. I didn't realize the magnitude of this gesture until I walked in—there were representatives from Palm, Canon, E-Bike (a hybrid multispeed bike and electric motorcycle), and assorted clothing companies. I was allowed to choose one item from each station and I ended up with an impressive goody bag for Christmas gifts. They were actually handing out Digital Elphs like they were Halloween candies. This was another example of free stuff for those who can actually afford to buy it.

One of Woodward's street courses.

The lovely Erin and her husband at the awards.

Mama said nothing about knocking me out. Me and L.L.

"it was a perfect way to end a Vegas getaway— bloody and broke"

I left and headed back to the hotel and got ready for the event, which involved getting dressed and picking up Erin from the airport. It was the first time she had left the house since Thanksgiving, and she was struggling to keep her nausea at bay. There was a mob of still photographers in one area who would call out the names of celebrities walking by and ask them to stop. I got caught in the mix, so Erin and I stood perplexed while trying to appease various shouts of "Look this way! Over here! To the right! Up here! Who is your friend? How do you spell her name? E, R, I . . . wait! There's Jessica Simpson! Jessica! Look over here!"

I was taken to the stage greenroom while everyone else went to a larger greenroom. **I SNUCK OUT AND JOINED THE OTHERS, MOSTLY TO BE WITH MY FRIENDS, BUT ALSO BECAUSE THEY HAD FOOD IN THEIR ROOM.** The show finally started and I headed back to the stage holding cell (aka greenroom) where anyone about to go onstage was hanging out—including Christina Aguilera (who was flanked by record execs), Oscar De La Hoya, L.L. Cool J, and Faith Hill. There was no place to sit, so I stood next to a monitor. I started talking to a guy who recognized me, and I learned that he was Christina's friend—although he wouldn't elaborate as to the extent of their friendship. I asked if I could get a picture with her, but it was impossible to get through the posse of yes-men that surrounded her.

It was finally my turn to present with Pink. I started panicking that I wouldn't be able to see the TelePrompTer and begged Pink to let me look at her copy. We walked out onstage, pausing a couple of times because Pink's dress kept getting stuck on her heels. I looked up and the TelePrompTer was easy to read, so I went through my lines without stalling. As we opened the winner of Best Rock Artist, the crowd was chanting "Creed" before we even got to read it, so I said it as if everyone already knew. The band came up and accepted while I snacked on the giant fortune cookie that the winning envelope came in. We all walked offstage and my job was finished.

★ ★ ★ ★ ★ ★ ★ ★ ★ ★ ★ ★ ★ ★ ★ ★ ★

At the next commercial break, I found my seat next to my friends while following No Doubt down the aisles. We watched the rest of the show while being entertained by a famous rap star's sarcastic commentary (he was right in front of us). As Britney Spears accepted her award with a gushing speech about how this is all a dream and she never wants to wake up, we overheard the rapper snicker and say, "Oh, you're gonna wake up" under his breath. The rest of the show was pretty generic. The whole event is based purely on sales, so it's really just an excuse for a bunch of megamarketers to pat themselves on the backs for jobs well done throughout the year.

As the show finished, we headed over to the Hard Rock Hotel for the after party. I didn't stay long. Matty and I filtered out to the casino while Erin headed back to the MGM with her longtime friend Nausea. I returned to the room a few hours later with nothing more than a few silver dollars to my name. I tossed them on the bed and exclaimed that it was all I had left. Erin grabbed one, claiming that they were heavy and actually hurt when one landed on her. She threw it at me, aiming for my chest but hit me in the middle of my forehead. Blood instantly dripped down my face and I then believed that these coins could actually inflict damage. I had no choice but to laugh hysterically and fall asleep with a washcloth draped over my face. It was a perfect way to end a Vegas getaway—bloody and broke.

★ ★ ★ ★ ★ ★

IN MEMORY OF RAYMOND LANG

DECEMBER 17, 2000
YMCA Skatepark: Mission Valley, California

About two weeks ago, a seventeen-year-old named Raymond Lang was skating with his friends in their neighborhood in San Diego. One of their neighbors, whose own son was also skating, came out, complaining that the kids were too close to his car. He had made the same complaint in the past and even threatened them with a BB gun the week before. This time he brought out a real shotgun and shot Raymond in the chest simply for skating in his own neighborhood. He then turned the gun on Raymond's younger brother and threatened him with "more of the same." Raymond died shortly after, and the raging lunatic now faces trial. **THERE IS NO WAY TO EXPRESS THE SADNESS OF THIS TRAGEDY AND THE IMPACT IT HAD ON THE SKATING COMMUNITY, ESPECIALLY IN OUR HOMETOWN.**

Ozzie—the director of the Mission Valley Y—took it upon himself to hold a fund-raiser for the family at the skatepark. The family is not well off and the funeral costs were another blow in an already impossible situation. Companies and skaters came out in droves for this cause and the event looked like something that had been planned months ahead of time. I showed up at 1 P.M. and started skating the vert ramp along with Bucky, Andy, Bob, Pierre-Luc, and Peter Hewitt.

I skated for almost an hour, and then met Raymond's family—his brother, mom, and stepdad. They were all wearing shirts with Raymond's school photo printed on the back. What can one say? Words cannot express this type of sorrow.

I signed autographs for about an hour, but I couldn't shake the sadness of why this whole event came together. This tragedy speaks of issues regarding gun control and skate harassment more than any other. We can only hope that some good will come of this in the form of better understanding, tolerance, and justice.

Ruden Tapeda is serving fifty years to life.

NO PARKING

[part 2] 2001

JACKASSED JANUARY 14, 2001

Jackass: Orlando, Florida

I was invited by Jeff Tremaine, the *Jackass* producer, to join the *Jackass* crew to witness/try a loop with Mat Hoffman. They had built a number of obstacles and launching ramps into and around a lake. They also built a sixteen-foot loop (two feet bigger than ones I have done) that curved to the right (I have only gone to the left, so this was frontside). We got there a little late, so Mat was already up on the starting ramp and the Jackasses themselves (Johnny Knoxville, Steve-O, Bam, Chris Pontius, Ryan Dunn, and Brandon Dicamillo) were preparing the crash pads.

I immediately put my pads on in order to warm up and give Mat support. He had never tried a loop before and wasn't sure how to go at it. He came in with too much speed and fell into the ramp just past twelve o'clock. One of the hardest things to figure out about doing a loop is that it doesn't require as much speed as it seems. Too much speed forces you into the wall with no hope of standing up. After about a half hour of attempts, Mat started to figure out the speed factor but not the aim. He kept coming around and ending up back in the starting ramp instead of carving toward the exit. I was trying to warm up in the meanwhile, but my attempts weren't consistent. I would come around perfectly into the pads on one and totally flail the next.

They removed the pad that blocked the exit and Mat made it through without any problems. I also made it after a few tries. The plan was to have us both wear chicken suits, follow each other through the loop, and launch into the lake. I tried to make it around again before donning the costume, but I bailed about halfway through and came down straight on my shin on the edge of the ramp. My shin was shredded from my kneepad to just above my ankle and probably could have used some stitches near the bottom. Luckily, Barry Zaritsky came along to check out the action and was a big help with cleaning the wound. I decided to quit, since I had already made it once.

Mat and I then suited up in full chicken gear. My plan was to jump in the lake at the same time as him, after he went through the loop. There was a starting ramp next to the exit of the loop, so I waited for him to come out and then dropped in. He made it perfectly, so I went down the ramp and ended up launching right next to him just after he took off. We flew into the water like the flightless chickens we emulated. It was *cold*, but I tried to play it off while swimming back to shore. I removed the damp suit, cleaned my shin one more time, got packed, and said good-bye. Riley and I had to catch a flight, since the next day was a school day. I fear for whatever shenanigans were in store for the crew once we left—we'll just have to wait for the show to air. I guess it was worth yet another shinner to be part of the hijinks that have become standard *Jackass* fodder, but it's really starting to hurt.

[Clockwise] The crew, the loop, and the chickens.

VENICE MEETS PARK CITY

JANUARY 19, 2001

Sundance Film Festival: Park City, Utah

I was invited to the annual Sundance Film Festival to attend a screening of *Dogtown and Z-Boys*, Stacy Peralta's documentary on the Dogtown skate team of the seventies. Vans financed the project and they brought it here in hopes of selling it to a major film distributor, which will allow it to be released widely in theaters. It is difficult to get a film into the festival since only a handful will get picked out of hundreds of entries. There was a huge buzz surrounding Stacy's film before it premiered, which is always a good sign.

Morgan, Matty, Mort, and I arrived in Salt Lake City with enough time to check out a new skate park (huge and fun, but no vert ramp) before driving up to Park City. We pulled in with minutes to spare before the film started and the place was packed. The theaters here are generally hotel ballrooms or offices converted into screening rooms, so there isn't much room for a crowd. If you're not a bigwig studio exec or haven't set up tickets way ahead of time, it's not likely that you'll get into a screening of a decent movie here. Matty and Mort didn't have passes, but we managed to squeak by the doorman with the help of Steve Van Doren (president of Vans, Inc).

THE DOCUMENTARY IS TRULY AMAZING. NARRATED BY SEAN PENN, IT COVERS AN ERA OF SKATING THAT MOST SKATERS TODAY ARE UN-AWARE EVER EXISTED. It details a group of surfers from the streets of Santa Monica that changed the world of skateboarding—Tony Alva, Jay Adams, Jim Muir, Jeff Ho, Shogo Kubo, and Stacy, to name a few. These guys began skating as it was being invented, and surfing inspired their styles and maneuvers. As the rest of the skating community focused on freestyle-based riding (360s, wheelies, handstands, and other flat-ground maneuvers), this unique and notoriously rowdy group chose to mimic their wave experience and ride empty swimming pools. Hence the birth of vert skating. It documents the group's rise to fame and subsequent breakup. I have a small interview in it, but I started skating just after this group disbanded, so I couldn't give a true fan's perspective. It is the most engaging documentary I've watched and it enlightened me on a revolutionary part of skating's history. It won two major awards at the festival, making it almost certain for theatrical release. All I can say is go see it if you have the chance.

MADTV

JANUARY 25, 2001

Fox Studios: Los Angeles, California

MadTV asked me to be on their show, so they wrote a sketch to include skating. The segment is an idea they have done before where a character named Will—a teenage kid—is always pestered by his little sister. He comes to see me perform and waits in line to get my autograph only to be embarrassed by his sister's insults. He tosses her aside and I "refuse to give an autograph to a bully." She continues to come back until I see his point of view because she starts in on me as well.

THE ENTIRE SHOOT ONLY TOOK ABOUT TWO HOURS and it was seriously hard not to laugh during our takes—theirs is a talented cast of comedians. I have had many offers to be on TV shows (*Letterman*, *Leno*, and the *Today* show for example), but they usually back out because they never want to go through the expense or hassle of getting a ramp to skate, so I appreciate Fox Television's making such an effort.

Filming for MadTV.
Fox never had a stage like this before.

THE WINTER X GAMES

JANUARY 31, 2001

New York City to Mount Snow, Vermont

I had some meetings in New York City yesterday, and Frank B., who runs the Jones Athlete Team, just happened to be there with the Jones Soda RV so we decided we would drive up to Vermont together. Robert Earl and Morgan met up with us, because they convinced ESPN that there should be a feature on our "road to X." It was more of an excuse for us to hang out together in the city, but it worked.

Last night Rob and Frank got a craving for doughnuts so we pulled the purple, flame-covered RV up to a Dunkin' Donuts. Once inside, the workers looked tired and overworked. Rob asked them what time they got to go home, but they were stuck there all night or until all the doughnuts were sold. Being good samaritans, Rob and Frank bought *every* doughnut in the store, which gave the workers an excuse to go home. They were so excited that they gave us gallons of milk and juice and all the plasticware we could carry. It cost a whopping forty dollars to shut the whole place down. We drove the streets of New York City giving doughnuts away to various pedestrians and homeless people until a group of kids started throwing them back at the RV. We declared war, and doughnuts were flying out of every window at our enemies. I hit one in the head with a jelly-filled just as we drove off. Needless to say, the RV was a mess at the end of the night.

We finally pulled into Mount Snow today around 10 P.M., shooting our faux segment all the way as we checked in.

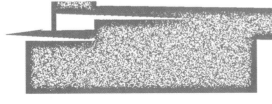

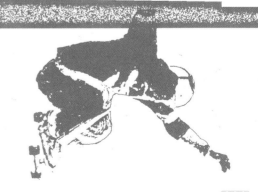

[Left] A signed X ray. Was it my fault?
[Right] Breakfast of Champions.

Champagne snorkel powder, bro. Double shaka!

★★★★★

The snowskate and the victim.

"i did an interview about entering the pro ranks at a young age"

★★★★★★★★★★★★★★★★★★★★★★★

FEBRUARY 4, 2001

I woke up and ran to the host set, since I was late for my only scheduled obligation of the day. I did an interview with Shaun Palmer about entering the pro ranks at a young age—we both turned pro when we were fourteen (Shaun White's age). They had old footage of us that they played in the background, which was entertaining and embarrassing at the same time. They also played our snowskate session from the first day out, which proved that Shaun White is the wonderboy of all board sports.

We were finished by 11 A.M., and I realized that all of my Winter X commitments were fulfilled. I've been here since the January 31. My flight home was scheduled for the next day and I was originally going to miss Erin's prenatal exam, but I scrambled to get my bags together and reschedule my flight to get home tonight. I pulled it off without a hitch thanks to United and made it home before midnight. I learned that a severe storm hit New England the next day and everyone else was stuck in Vermont for another two days. That would not have gone over well at home.

Frontside ollie, somewhere in Texas.

OLD-SCHOOL SKATE JAM

FEBRUARY 10, 2001

Skatelab Skate Park: Simi Valley, California

With all the buzz surrounding the Dogtown documentary, the owners of Skatelab Skatepark decided to invite all of the "old-school" skaters for a private session/party. Mort, Riley, and I drove up early in hopes of beating the crowds that were expected to arrive. We skated about twenty minutes before they officially opened the doors to the rest of the invitees. The bowl was instantly swarming with faces that I had not seen in twenty years; many I had only read about in magazines. The session started getting dangerous as up to three guys dropped in at once, but everyone managed to survive. Tony Alva, Art Dickey, Steve Cathey, Doug Saladino, Mike Folmer, Brad Bowman, and Steve Olson were just a few of the recognizable skaters on hand. I saw Alan Gelfand walk by and I introduced him to Riley as the guy who invented the ollie—I even got him to sign my board.

I JOINED IN THE BOWL MELEE AFTER IT CALMED SLIGHTLY. Someone else dropped in on my first run, so I stayed in the shallow end playing the who-will-bail-first game. I looked up as I was doing an axle stall and realized that it was my childhood skating hero, Eddie Elguera, skating the deep end. I immediately stopped and watched with the same excitement as when I was twelve. In fact, the whole night felt like my younger days, since it was all the same guys that used to intimidate me, vying to get a run and snaking me in the process. However, it was much more fun to be in the mix this time around.

Riley had a blast skating the street course with the local rippers until I finally had to convince him to leave for our long drive home. I tried to introduce him to most of the skaters I admired as a kid, but I don't think he really understood the importance of their generation. It's scary to think that in the not-so-distant future there will be an old-school gathering that will include all of the pros with whom I skate now. Riley could be there telling his friends about how he was inspired by this generation and showing us how much skating has evolved.

HAWK SKATE STORE
GRAND OPENING MARCH 17, 2001
Garden State Plaza: Paramus, New Jersey

The quest for autographs has gotten out of hand. I am beginning to get discouraged with public appearances that don't involve skating, simply because the demand for signatures is too big and I don't have the ability as a human being to fulfill them all. I now feel like I disappoint more people than I please at these events, which is the opposite of what I want to accomplish.

Case in point: today was the official grand opening of the first Hawk Skate retail store.

We arrived at the mall on schedule, and I made my way to a stage where they were holding a raffle. **THEY WERE GIVING OUT A TON OF PRIZES, WHICH INCLUDED SHIRTS, DECKS, AND A CHANCE TO GET AUTOGRAPHS INSIDE THE STORE (TWO HUNDRED IN TOTAL).** I walked up to the stage to an amazingly vocal, warm welcome from the crowd and proceeded to answer various questions (half being requests to shake hands). I signed every raffle item and then made my way to the side of the stage, where things got ugly. I tried to sign the multitude of products pushed in front of me, but it started getting dangerous with smaller kids getting crushed in the front.

There was no way to give everyone a signature without staying all day and missing the chance to give them a skating demo. I believe that people would actually like to see live skating instead of waiting hours for the hope of one autograph. I may be misguided in that belief these days, but I'd still like to think that it's the truth. I gave up and made my way to the store. People kept shoving things in front of my face to the point where I literally had no room to even hold up a pen and sign the stuff. One of the security guards told me that he got hit in the head with skateboards three times in our short trek.

At the store, the raffle winners soon started to trickle in. I was still frazzled by the previous debacle, but I was quickly touched at the heartfelt joy these kids showed once they approached me. I signed posters and took pictures for about two hours with the excited winners. We left the store through a back door, and headed straight to RexPlex for what I hoped would be the main reason people came to our event—to see some skating.

Frontside stiffy, Atlanta, GA.

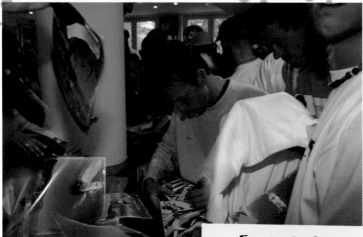

Store signings can get hectic.

We got there and the place was packed. I thought it was a great demo . . . except that I couldn't make a kickflip Indy for the life of me (I haven't missed that many since I learned them). Richard Lopez and I attempted some 900s, but I finally gave in to the fact that the ramp is too small for such a feat.

There was a large grouping of kids (and their parents) standing by the stairs asking for autographs every time I bailed and walked back up the ramp. They were standing in an area where they could see absolutely no action, begging for signatures for at least an hour. If I were to stop and sign their goods, I would have been surrounded by countless others and not been able to skate anymore. At one point I asked some of them if they realized that we were skating—and even trying 900s—on the very ramp that they were standing behind. None of them seemed to care. Have autographs (or merely the prospect of getting one) replaced the excitement of live demonstrations? It was never so apparent, and I don't understand this philosophy. Has it always been there, and I didn't notice because it was never on this scale? Are these die-hard autograph seekers only trying to make a profit on eBay? There may be no easy answers to these questions, but I feel the need to reevaluate. I would much rather skate than sign autographs, because that is what got me here in the first place—it is where I feel comfortable and in control. The whole autograph thing has become too important in the eyes of some fans and it is disheartening, mainly because it is impossible to please everyone. I don't mean to dwell, but something has to change and I'm not sure where the compromise lies.

WHERE'S BAM?

APRIL 2, 2001

Adio Tour: San Juan, Puerto Rico

We got here at 3 A.M. after an eighteen-hour nightmare trip. Our flight from San Diego was supposed to leave at 6:30 A.M. Kevin and I showed up with a half hour to spare (or so we thought) to find out that the flight had already left. I stood there arguing with a United representative that we still had time to make the flight until Jeff Taylor, the Adio team manager, came over to clear things up—we forgot about the time change. Duh. The saddest part is that out of the three of us, nobody accounted for it until it was too late. A very helpful woman at the check-in went out of her way to get us on another flight—a much later one—that still got us in with enough time to make our scheduled appearances. Bam was flying out from Los Angeles, and I just knew that he would run into the same problem. When we finally got into San Juan, Kenny Anderson and Jeremy Wray had arrived as scheduled (because they are much smarter than we are), but no sign of or message from Bam.

We arrived at the first shop to a buzzing crowd and a lot of cheering. The first kid came up to get signatures and asked, "Where's Bam?" This became the question of the day, to which we had no answer. We signed stuff for an hour and the line never seemed to get shorter. We finally had to leave in order to make it to our other appearances. Kids surrounded our van as we left the parking lot and pounded on the windows until I was convinced that they were going to shatter.

Ellis, Banny, Bam, and Bucky feeling it.

105

Bam, me, Kevin, Jeremy, and Kenny—fish out of water in Puerto Rico.

The next two shops were also in a mall—strangely, in the *same* mall. The distributors didn't want to leave any account hanging, so they committed to both for a half hour each. The first shop was the definition of chaos. The waiting crowd was pushed up right against the shop's window (about twelve feet high by twenty feet wide) and it started to bend from the pressure. It was a calamity waiting to happen. **NEEDLESS TO SAY, THIS WAS ANOTHER AUTOGRAPH SESSION THAT GOT CUT SHORT.**

As we pulled out of the mall parking lot with hordes of kids chasing our vehicle (and nearly getting run over), there was finally a message from Bam. He had to stay overnight in Houston because of the time-change fiasco and catch another flight. He had arrived in San Juan and had been waiting at the airport for nearly three hours. His cell phone was broken, and that was where he had all of his contacts stored (exactly why we hadn't heard from him). We pulled up to the baggage claim to find him sitting on the curb after his thirty-three-hour journey.

APRIL 3, 2001

We drove to a nearby military base on which there was a seemingly misplaced skate shop in a residential neighborhood. We exited the van to another vocal welcome and went straight to the autograph table, our second home. It was hectic.

One of the most amusing aspects of being on tour with Bam is that so many people know him from MTV instead of recognizing him as a pro skater. Kids would yell, "Do *Jackass*!" everywhere we went. Huh? What exactly does that mean? I suggested that if he stuck his finger down his throat and puked on them and it could pass for "doing *Jackass*."

There was a rumor about a good swell hitting in the morning and I would feel cheated going to Puerto Rico for the first time without surfing at all.

APRIL 4, 2001

The rumors were true. Juancarlos, our tour organizer, and Rick, Danny Montoya, and I grabbed surfboards and paddled way out to an empty reef break. It was a good wave, but we had to take off right near some big, exposed rocks, which made things intimidating for me. You don't find many spots like that in Southern California. I caught a few waves before finding myself washed up on a shallow reef after one closed out on me. Luckily, I didn't hit anything sharp and paddled back out before another set wave pushed me farther into the danger zone. I caught a couple more before paddling in. Then we were off to our demo.

When we got the skate shop, the plan was to do a street demo before hitting the vert ramp, but that plan was crushed as soon as we pulled up to the site. The abundant crowd spilled over into the surrounding streets, covering the designated street course area. So we moved to the vert ramp.

We skated for an hour and everything went well. Bam even "did *Jackass*" by jumping into a nearby tree from the deck of the ramp. He nearly fell onto his head on a cement wall about five feet below when the tree swung back from his weight. He held tight as it swung around, and was released onto his feet on the other side of the tree. The crowd instantly surrounded him and it looked like a killing scene from a *National Geographic*—I was waiting for him to be eaten alive and left for vulture scrap. It was genuinely scary, and I suggested that Jeff go pull him out of harm's way. After grabbing him we made a beeline to our cars. Bam tried to close the sliding door of our van, but there was a girl in an SUV next to us with her door open, intentionally blocking our door so it could not latch shut. Our van was surrounded by this time and it was looking like we were trapped. Bam tried to shut it again by slamming it harder, but only did more damage to the girl's door. He started yelling at her to close her door, but she stood there stoic and indifferent to our situation. Finally, Jeff realized he could back up and leave our nemesis's blockade behind.

We finally got back to our hotel—tired, hungry, and flustered. Kevin Staab, Bam, and I had to leave the next day in order to make it back for the ESPN Action Sports & Music Awards in L.A. No . . . sleep . . . till . . . Carlsbad.

(LIFETIME) ACHIEVEMENT AWARD APRIL 7, 2001

ESPN Action Sports & Music Awards: Los Angeles, California

The powers that be at ESPN took it upon themselves to create the first big televised awards show focusing exclusively on skateboarding and other "action" sports (formerly known as "extreme" sports). The date was set long ago to accommodate the many conflicting schedules of the honored athletes. When they first told me about the event, they said they wanted to present me with the first "action sports lifetime achievement award." They later omitted the "lifetime" part, as it suggested that my career (and future honorees' careers) had come to an end. Besides, I always picture lifetime achievement awards going to fragile old men who are barely able to read their own acceptance speeches and who stopped performing their craft long ago. The decision to change the title wasn't mine, but I was secretly relieved.

When we got to the venue, I was extremely nervous, knowing that my award could be up at any minute and that I would have to give an acceptance speech. I had a list of people to thank and I had a looming paranoia that I was going to forget someone important.

The moment came and Tom Green introduced my award. I was thankful that he took a break from editing his movie (the week before its release) to come and do this. Matty and Morgan from 900 Films had produced a special video segment that they wouldn't let me see until this event, but I didn't really get to see it even then due to the drunken skaters filling the aisle next to me, wanting to reminisce with me about old times. There were production people trying earnestly to make them move because I was supposed to get up and accept my award at any second, and a fight nearly ensued during what was supposed to be a happy occasion. I FINALLY MADE MY WAY TO THE STAGE, SHOOK TOM'S HAND, AND STARTED IN ON MY THANK-YOUS. I was suddenly stricken with the worst cast of cottonmouth, and felt compelled to continually lick my lips to keep them from sticking to my "tOM gReeN inTRoDucEd mY aWaRd"

gums. I struggled through the names on my list, glancing down once in a while in hopes of not leaving anyone out. It is frightening to be alone on a stage like that, knowing that it is your one chance to give gratitude to the people who have influenced your life. I finished and walked offstage with Tom when it dawned on me: I forgot to thank my mom. She was on the list! I swear! In fact, she was the first name in my list of family. I guess I didn't look at my list enough, or maybe it was the chatty aisle-dwellers, or maybe I needed a drink of water, or maybe I was too nervous, or maybe . . . I just blew it.

LUCKILY, I HAVE TWO OTHER AWARDS SHOWS TO ATTEND IN THE NEXT COUPLE WEEKS AND GOOD CHANCES FOR REDEMPTION.

I made it back to my seat and my mom was sitting next to Erin. I apologized in hopes that they hadn't noticed my acceptance speech faux pas, but of course it was already a topic of discussion before I even returned. If there is one mom who would not be fazed by such a thing, it's mine.

Getting ready at the Mondrian: Jen, Bam, Matty, Cathy, and Juliette Lewis (in background).

sPeeCh

"I would first like to thank ESPN for giving skateboarding so much recognition and support over recent years, and for giving us a medium to display our talents. I would also like to thank them for no longer using the word 'extreme.' On a personal level, I wish to thank everyone that has believed in me over the years—my ever-supportive family (Mom, Steve, Pat, Lenore), my beautiful wife and hottest MILF around (Erin), my sons Riley and Spencer. Everyone at Birdhouse and Blitz; Sarah Hall Productions; Brian Dubin and the crew at William Morris; Jared, Ray, and Kevin at THI; Morgan and Matty at 900 Films; Activision; Neversoft; Stacy Peralta; and the Chin Brigade. I would like to thank the fans of skateboarding everywhere, but thanks most of all to my father, who could have never imagined that driving his son to the skatepark every day would amount to this. This one's for you, Dad."

"this one's for you, dad"

" I aCCepTed mY awArD aNd OpEned mY spEEch by thanking My mOm "

THANKS, MOM! APRIL 10, 2001

Blockbuster Awards: Los Angeles, California

'Tis the season for awards shows, and L.L. Cool J is at every single one. The Blockbuster Awards were originally reserved for movies and their popularity based on number of rentals. They stretched it this year to include categories such as video games, which is where I fit into the picture. They wanted me to present an award, and introduce me as the winner of all three video game categories: favorite PlayStation, Dreamcast, and Game Boy games. They also wanted me to jump through a large sheet of paper for my entrance, which I rehearsed a couple days in advance.

They were going to project skate and gameplay footage on the paper and wanted me to come through it at just the right time. I was to go straight to the podium and accept my awards from Frankie Muniz (Malcolm from *Malcolm in the Middle*). None of this was a problem until I got backstage for the real thing and realized that I was wearing my dress shoes.

In the rush of getting ready, I forgot about my skating obligation on the show and didn't even bring my skate shoes. Luckily, my Prada shoes are not the dressiest and have fairly sticky soles. I rolled around backstage minutes before my scheduled entrance, practicing ollies and destroying the

side of my new shoes. They worked okay, but I wouldn't have wanted to try anything else in them.

The time came and I busted through the "screen" on cue. I realized later that if I had bailed and my board shot out, it would have taken out one or more of the following celebrities in the front row: Ricky Martin, Christina Aguilera, Cameron Diaz, Lucy Liu, Drew Barrymore, Tom Green, Dustin Hoffman, Annette Bening, or any member of *NSync.

I accepted my award and opened my speech by thanking my mom. Ahhh . . . redemption.

I went back to my seat, when a frantic stage producer asked if Dustin Hoffman could borrow my skateboard. Huh? Things are very strange lately. Dustin was presenting the World Artist Award to his good friend Warren Beatty, and he wanted to skate onstage. Having no idea if he could even skate, I was now convinced that someone from *NSync would go home with a bloody lip from my board hitting him. Dustin came out and it was obvious that he actually could skate, but he was trying to act like he couldn't. At one point, he almost fell back and shot the board out, nearly making my boy-band-bashing vision a reality. For the record, Dustin Hoffman pushes mongo-footed. He and Warren signed my board when they were finished.

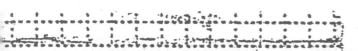

CHOCOLATE MONSTER

APRIL 21, 2001

Nickelodeon Kids' Choice Awards: Los Angeles, California

The Kids' Choice Awards is an annual Nickelodeon event where kids vote for their favorite people in various categories. I was up for Favorite Male Athlete (along with Shaq, Kobe Bryant, and Tiger Woods—whoa!) and Favorite Video Game. They asked if I would skate out to the podium and present an award with Ray Romano.

We had to arrive early, because they wanted Riley to skate out with me to the podium and we needed to rehearse the timing. It was a setup for Ray Romano to do a gag with his kids as well. When we got there, I was informed that I won both categories (I still find it unbelievable that I received more votes than the other athletes did) and I would need to give an acceptance speech before doing the bit with Ray.

Ray Romano and family. Spencer enjoys a soda, oblivious to his surroundings.

[Top left] Spencer [pre-barf] and a girl band [name?].
[Top right] Corralling the chocolate demon.
[Bottom] DVDs are essential kid entertainment for long trips.

We spent time between rehearsals in the greenroom taking advantage of the bountiful snacks. Spencer was particularly excited, because we usually keep him away from candy. He was pouring cupfuls of M&Ms into his mouth between bites of brownies and lollipops. I noticed that he was having a hard time swallowing these gigantic mouthfuls of chocolate, as brown drool oozed from the corners of his mouth. Suddenly, I saw him running to a nearby table where there were a few members of the Baha Men who were acting like he was holding a grenade. I went over and realized that he had barfed chocolate all over himself, wiping it with his hands and smearing it all over his face and shirt. People were scattering to get away from him and he thought it was a game, so he went running wild chasing them, laughing the whole time. Erin tried to catch him, but it was like trying to corral a muddy piglet at a wedding reception. She finally caught him, which only made him laugh harder. Luckily, we'd brought a change of clothes for the chocolate monster and managed to keep the black goo off anyone else. It was one of the funniest chase scenes I've ever witnessed.

Ray and I did our "routine" and then presented the award for Favorite Male Singer to Lil' Bow Wow, who was born for show business. After the show ended we made our way upstream (against the masses) to the backstage area and the after party.

Spencer was falling apart from his sugar-induced jitters, and I was immersed in signing autographs while trying to calm my inconsolable two-year-old. It was not an easy walk to the exit. We finally found everyone and headed home—Spencer instantly passed out in the car. THE KIDS HAD A BLAST—NICKELODEON KNOWS HOW TO CATER A SHOW AND PARTY TO THEM.

The Nickelodeon slime button.

Demonstrating the ollie. I almost fell on my butt when I landed due to the slimy floor.

THE (INTERNATIONAL) GIGANTIC SKATEPARK TOUR APRIL 25, 2001

San Francisco, California, to London, England

We arrived last night after a six-hour flight delay in San Francisco. Almost everyone was on the flight from San Francisco to London (Kris Markovich, Bucky Lasek, Morgan, Matty, Rooftop, Jason Ellis, Sal Masakela, Ian Votteri, and the production crew), so I felt sorry for the flight attendants. Some of our crew even managed to sneak into business class halfway through the flight.

Doing a European leg of the Gigantic Skatepark Tour was a difficult project to get approved. We made a skimpy schedule (three stops total) in hopes that the cost would not be an issue. We still didn't know if it was on as of two weeks before our departure date, so we were pleasantly surprised when our double-decker bus pulled in to the airport to pick us up. Bam Margera, Steve Berra, and Mat Hoffman were already onboard after flying straight here from the Louisville B3 event.

We left the hotel in the bus and went to see Big Ben and Buckingham Palace—true tourists on a mission. We shot some *Reservoir Dogs* group shots in front of each landmark before our next excursion: paintball wars. I have never played with paintball guns before, but I have seen the welts that getting shot can produce on your skin.

It took nearly two hours to get there, and it was the first time I'd slept for more than an hour since arriving in England. We divided into two teams (mine consisted of Ellis, Hoffman, Bam, and Rick Thorne) and went out to a wooded area with various forts and barricades to hide in/behind.

We played three games, each in different areas where the object was to capture the other team's flag. If you get shot anywhere besides your head, you are out. We won the first game by default because Thorne was the only soldier left without getting hit. I got hit in the shoe, so I avoided the dreaded sting. I was not so lucky on the second outing—I peaked my head out from over a wall only to see "bullets" coming at me. One hit me in the goggles so I decided to take cover, but it was too late. Another hit me on the side of my head right below the safety mask we were required to wear. It seriously hurt. I sat on my knees in the mud cursing this whole idea. I went out and managed to hit Bucky in the leg before getting tagged in the back by Rooftop.

The bus crew en route. Europe never knew what hit it. From left to right: Ryan Young, Morgan Stone, Robert Earl, Bucky Lasek, Jared Prindle, Matty Goodman, moi, Trent Kamerman, Rick Thorne, and [Sweet] Frank Barbara.

"We sTill diDn't knOw if iT wAs on aS of tWo weeks befOre our dEparture daTe, so We weRe pleAsantly SurpRised whEn our DOUBLE-DECKER bUs pullEd In to tHe AirpOrt to picK us Up"

Look kids—Big Ben and the Houses of Parliament!

The last game put our team on the offense, trying to capture the other team's flag from a fortress. I snuck around the side and got into a back-and-forth gunfight with Bucky, who was hiding behind a barrier and managed to fit his gun barrel through the slats. I heard his gun firing empty shots after a while, and I realized that he needed to reload. I took the chance and ran into the middle of the fortress, thinking that the flag was near the flagpole and I could go in commando style. I should have surveyed the location from the front because the flag was nowhere in sight and I was a sitting duck firing wildly at no visible enemies. I got tagged on both hands, neither of which were covered and it stung like hell, and numerous times in the face mask. One bullet exploded right on the air holes of the mask, and I could taste paint shooting into my mouth. Bad idea. As I walked out in surrender-position, I saw the flag lying right at the entrance. It could have been so easy. Ellis tried a similar move to mine, but he slid out in the mud right as he reached the flag and got pelted too many times to count. **OUR TIME WAS UP AND WE WERE THE DEFEATED TROOP.**

As the other team was firing victory shots in the air, I snuck up on Robert Earl and nailed him in the calf. I was suddenly a fugitive desperately looking for the border (exit), as their entire army (Rob, Rooftop, Bucky, Sal, Berra, and Frank) chased me through the woods. I was shooting backwards in hopes of hitting anyone during the chase. I only got hit a couple of times, once in the back and once on my butt. One of my blind shots got Rob, so it was a worthwhile effort. After getting hit that many times in exposed areas, I understand all the fuss about getting stung. Those little balls of paint actually break skin.

When Ellis Attacks.

"we shot some Reservoir Dogs group shots in front of each landmark"

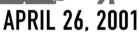

APRIL 26, 2001

I woke up early to do our first of many interviews for the tour. I then went to a radio station across the street (it was BBC 1,2,3 . . . or 7, I can't remember) to do a taped interview. I sat in an empty room after being told to put on the headphones and did an interview with the voice being piped into my head—I never saw anyone, except the person who showed me into the room. I was then supposed to meet a newspaper reporter at a nearby sushi restaurant, but I got lost trying to find it. Never try to give a Yankee directions around a city like London. I grabbed a cup of soup to go and made it back to the hotel right at 2:30 P.M., just as our bus was leaving for the skatepark.

We actually got to the park on time. I still can't get used to going to a skatepark cold turkey and being expected to perform at a top level. We cruised around the abundant street course for a few minutes, figuring out what it had to offer and how to get speed on the rough asphalt surface. **I WAS LESS THAN FIFTEEN MINUTES INTO SKATING WHEN I TWISTED MY BACK ANKLE.** After landing another trick to fakie, I tried to do a cab melon over the only spine there. I misjudged the landing, went to the flat, my foot came off the board, and I ran over it. It was a substantial sprain, but not as bad as I have done to my other ankle many more times. I had to make a quick decision as to whether or not to persevere and continue skating or submit to Barry and the endless icings he inevitably would require. Getting treated meant missing the rest of the street demo and making it to the vert demo if I was lucky. Even Barry agreed that I should continue skating and pay the price later. I kept going but it was a struggle—my ankle was tightening up by the minute, and I was quickly losing all of my pop. I managed to tailslide a decent-sized ledge and make a few other transfers before cutting out and confronting the Ice Man.

My ankle was already noticeably swollen when I got into the bus. Barry wrapped it in ice for nearly thirty minutes and then taped it to the hilt. I could barely move it when I finally got to the vert ramp (the demo already in progress), partly because of the sprain, but mostly because of the precautionary taping Barry had provided. **THE RAMP WAS SMALL, BARELY TEN FEET, MAKING FOR A VERY CHALLENGING DEMO.** I managed a few good runs between lots of ankle pain–induced bails. There was some seriously good riding going on, namely by Bucky, Ali Cairns (who made a guest appearance), and Simon Tabron (world-class BMXer). Simon pulled a perfect 900 on the less-than-perfect ramp and Ali made his signature cab to five-0 to backside tailslide to revert. Bucky started trying nollie kickflip to backside tailslide (his latest invention), so I decided to go for a frontside gay twist body-varial (my newest). Either the ramp was too small or my ankle was too jacked, but it wasn't working. I opted to try a 360 varial gay twist, but it was still a struggle. The demo came down to Bucky and me flailing our chosen vices, until I finally gave up. I ended with a 540 run (doing different variations), and tried to finally make the 360 varial gay twist at the end. I caught it, threw it on the wall, squatted through the flat, and slid out on the other wall. Good enough, I guess. Bucky made his super-tech trick a few tries later, and then made another on the same run for good measure. It was a great ending and the crowd was going off. I limped my way through the autograph seekers and finally got on the bus. Barry was right there, ice in hand.

"i still can't get used to going to a skatepark cold turkey and being expected to perform at a top level"

APRIL 27, 2001

London, England, to Paris, France

We spent the entire day on the bus (with the exception of two hours on a ferry) driving to Paris. For nearly eight hours, Barry iced my ankle every forty minutes for twenty minutes at a time. Everyone else got into their old tour-bus habits by playing blackjack and watching movies. I got to play a few hands with Trent, our tried-and-true dealer, but icing my ankle was Barry's focus and there was no rest for the wicked. We arrived at the Paris Hilton (located right next to the Eiffel Tower) around 11 P.M. This was just the beginning of the night for many of the crew, but my day had been long enough.

Omar and I prepare for battle.

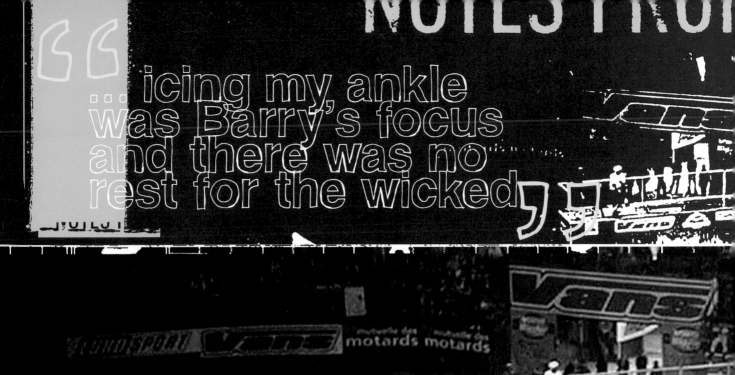

"... icing my ankle
was Barry's focus
and there was no
rest for the wicked"

The view from the crowd—Bercy, Gay
Paris.

APRIL 28, 2001
Vans Big Air: Paris, France

We spent most of the day driving around Paris (in the rain) and getting our tourism on. We did intros for the show right in front of the Eiffel Tower before going to Bercy Stadium for the annual Vans Big Air event. This is my fourth year in a row doing the event, but this year they did a cross-promotion with the tour.

We pulled up to the stadium where there are some good-sized ledges and a huge grass hill that was dangerously steep—perfect obstacles for our crew. Kris and Rooftop wanted to conquer the biggest ledge, but there was a small car in the way of the landing. The larger half of our posse bounced it out of the way. They tried it, but the takeoff and landing were a little too wet.

We went in, and I started to worry about what I would be able to do with a stiff ankle on a ramp that I have never skated, with no warm-up, in front of ten thousand people. At least we were scheduled for two demos throughout the night, so there was a chance to get used to the ramp. I struggled through the first demo, and it was not fun. I should have at least made time to skate the ramp earlier in the day to figure out the transitions and coping before going out cold turkey. One wall was over-vert and would pitch you out to the flat if you weren't prepared for it. Bucky didn't seem to have any of these problems and was killing it. I was just starting to get used to it and my ankle was feeling looser when they shut off the lights on the vert ramp, indicating the motocross big air event was underway.

Bonjour! Je m'appelle Tony.

We hung out backstage for an hour while they did the moto stuff and pom-pom dances (by cheer-leaders in illegal outfits). We went out again and the ramp was feeling better, but I was still bailing on stuff that I usually have wired. I did an Indy 360 on the ominous wall without compensating for the over-vert, landed way too low, and went straight to my elbow and hip. When it rains it pours in regard to my injuries. I stayed by the side of the ramp feigning that it didn't hurt that much, but my elbow was pounding. This kind of thing only pisses me off and makes me want to skate harder, so I went back up to the ramp. I did a couple of decent runs and decided to chuck a 900 attempt for the crowd. The over-vert wall was actually an advantage on a ramp this size, since it pitched me out enough to spin all the way. I tried it again and missed the grab, but I have learned recently (the hard way) not to worry about where my board is and just get around to my knees. I heard my board hit the ramp very near my head as I was sliding. I tried a few more and started getting a good spin.

Suddenly the spotlights moved away from the ramp and the motorcycles came out. I guess the or-ganizer's schedule had to run like clockwork. There was still enough light on the ramp, so I kept going. They had turned the ramp announcer's mike off, which meant he couldn't explain to the audience what was going on. I tried a few more, nearly squatted one out, and finally made it standing up. The crowd's reaction was deafening; I didn't know it at the time, but the moto guys had stopped riding and came over to the ramp to watch. Anyway, I was stoked to redeem myself after a less-than-impressive demo. The main organizer asked me to give a speech to the crowd, so **I THANKED EVERYONE IN MY BEST FRENCH AND WE BAILED OUT.**

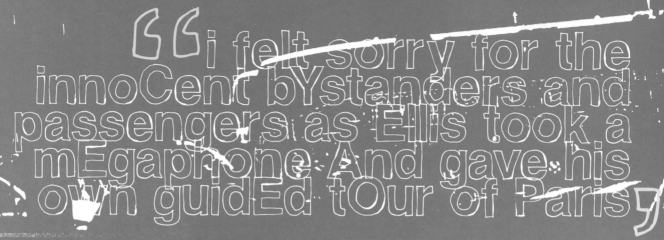

"i felt sorry for the innoCent bYstanders and passengers as Ellis took a mEgaphone And gave his own guidEd tOur of Paris"

ILE DE FRANCE

I feel sorry for the genuine tourists that get caught in our wake.

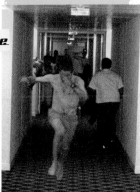

APRIL 29, 2001

Spent most of the day redoing the rainy intros and tourist stops for the cameras. We took a riverboat around the city with everyone piled in. I felt sorry for the innocent bystanders and passengers as Ellis took a megaphone and gave his own guided tour of Paris. I felt even more sorry for the couple we caught making out under a bridge, as all twenty of us—skaters, bikers, and production crew—heckled them from a boat only twenty feet away.

It was the mellowest night we'd had until Rooftop got an idea involving the megaphone. He had been sharing a room with Barry and had countless complaints about Barry's tidiness, so it was payback time. He wanted to turn the microphone's siren function on as Barry slept, and wake him as if there was a fire in the hallway. Suddenly, most of our crew congregated in the lobby, bored of being in their rooms and too used to our schedule to go to sleep. We formulated a plan that involved everyone: As Barry woke up in a haze and opened the door, he would see the rest of us running through the hallway (many half-dressed) and freak. We even had a random guy in the bar join in on the joke, since he was familiar with our tour shows (he's a skater's dad from Lake Tahoe). Berra and Thorne stripped down to their underwear for a convincing effect. ROOFTOP SET UP TWO CAMERAS IN THE ROOM AND TURNED THE THING ON. THERE WERE ABOUT TWELVE OF US IN THE HALLWAY RUNNING IN A PANIC, AND I WATCHED BARRY AS HE LOOKED OUT THE DOOR, ASSESSED THE SITUATION, AND MADE A BEELINE FOR THE STAIRS (WHERE EVERYONE WAS WAITING). HE SAW MY FACE FIRST AND REALIZED IT WAS A JOKE. He turned around with a dazed smirk on his face, nodded in defeat and went back to his room. The funniest thing, which I only realized later, was that Kris and Bam came out running in their underwear and were never in on the joke. Kris opened his door to check out the commotion, saw our ringer (the guy from Tahoe) and was convinced that this was for real. We all went to Bucky's room and checked the footage—hilarious. Faking a fire drill is a federal offense in the U.S., so I wouldn't recommend it. I'm not sure what the case is on the other side of the Atlantic, but luckily nobody else was awakened by our scheme.

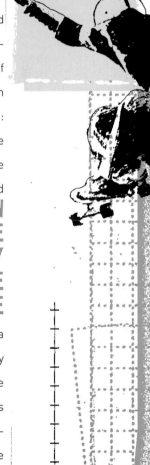

MAY 1, 2001
Frankfurt, Germany

After a full day of driving, we arrived at our hotel in Frankfurt. We checked into the hotel and headed to the demo earlier than expected because of Mayday protests and potential riots or roadblocks along the way. The crowd at "Railslide Hall" (how Euro) was smaller than predicted—there were fire code issues with the skatepark, so only a certain number were allowed in. The street demo went off with Steve, Bam, and Kris utilizing every obstacle. It is the best-designed street course I've seen in Europe, and would rival most U.S. parks. I spent most of the time on the side of the course with bigger (read: vert) stuff, feeling very squirrelly for some reason. About twenty minutes into skating, just as I was losing the shaky feeling, I did an impossible up and over a bank-to-deck transfer. I landed it, but started leaning too far to the edge of the box. I decided to drop off instead of bailing even though I was turned a little sideways. It would have worked out fine, but I forgot that the floor was very slippery. Instead of landing on the ground and adjusting my angle, my board slid out unexpectedly. I could feel my front foot folding as I fell to my side and the awful truth set in: I had sprained my other ankle. When it pours, it floods.

My right foot is more prone to sprains, since I have sprained it much worse and more times than my left. Right away I could tell that it wasn't too bad. I probably could have kept skating, but I felt like I had done everything I wanted to on the street course and didn't want to risk making it worse. I spent another street demo finale in the bus with ice on my ankle, trying to get motivated to skate vert.

I went up to the ramp with both ankles taped up and started warming up with Bucky, Jason, Mat, Thorne, and a few locals. We were all having trouble with the ramp because it was deceiving—it had big transitions, a good surface, and everything you'd expect from a good vert ramp . . . except enough vert.

Skating a 13-foot ramp with less than two feet of vert is similar to skating a miniramp because you hang up on every air, and every trick requires a huge ollie. We were bailing left and right on very basic tricks because of the lack of vert. The crowd was unusually quiet during the street demo and their disposition didn't improve with our vert struggle. Bucky and I got the loudest cheer with a short doubles routine. We then moved the crowd away from one side to try a vert-to-miniramp transfer that was about twelve feet across. I did it in a few tries because it was frontside for me, which is much easier to see the landing. Ellis tried it a few times (backside), but couldn't get the right take-off angle. Bucky and Mat made it a few tries later, officially marking the end of our European Skatepark Tour.

The street guys skated another two hours for their own pleasure. This crowd wasn't overwhelming, so it was the first time on this year's tour that I came out for an autograph session. We finally dragged Berra from the street course and went back to the hotel. Most of the guys fabricated a blackjack table in one of the hotel's conference rooms, but I'd had enough on the bus and called it a night.

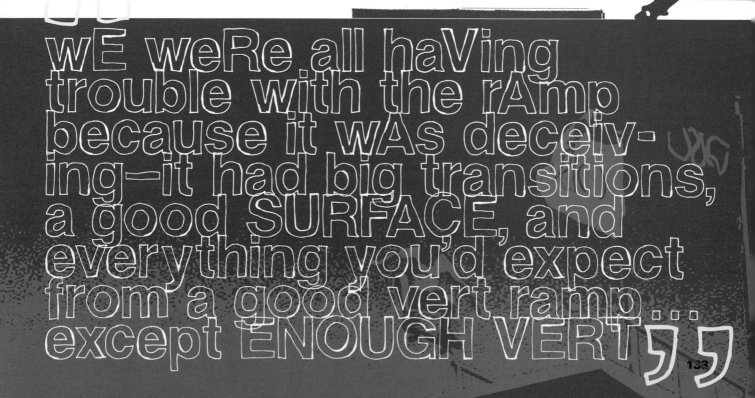

wE weRe all haVing trouble with the rAmp because it wAs deceiving—it had big transitions, a good SURFACE, and everything you'd expect from a good vert ramp... except ENOUGH VERT...

MAY 2, 2001
Frankfurt, Germany

The plan for our one day off in Frankfurt was for go-karts. This place was serious, with electronic lap timing and thirty minute rallies. I was just behind Mat, Ellis, and Thorne for most of the race. Thorne took the title in the end, but Ellis got the most respect for spinning out twice and still managing to almost win. I finished fourth, less than a second behind Mat "The Condor" Hoffman.

This was by far the most successful outing of our Gigantic Skatepark project and it barely came together. Thanks to the powers that be for finally approving our global vision for the tour and to the crew that sacrificed skin, sleep, and family for coming along. It was a blast, and it has only just begun for this year. Next, we go to Texas on May 21 to start the West Coast leg of the Gigantic Skatepark Tour.

A fourteen-foot ramp + crane = six-foot rail.
Backside 50-50 in a construction zone.

Gentlemen, start your egos.

KEEGAN WESLEY ANSON HAWK JULY 18, 2001

Scripp's Memorial Hospital: La Jolla, California

Our skatepark tour happened earlier this year because Erin was due with our second child (my third). She was only four days overdue, but I was on high alert because her previous labor was only four hours from start to finish. The time came, but getting her to leave the house might have been more labor for me than what she was about to go through. Her water had already broke and she wandered around the house tidying up and collecting various "necessities" for the hospital. We were way too cliché, speeding down the freeway in the midnight hour with her breathing through contractions. Some dude in a slick car thought I was trying to race him and made every effort to weave around slower traffic for his ultimate victory. If he only knew what was happening in his "opponent's" car . . .

We got to the hospital and Keegan was born less than an hour later. No anesthesia, just lots of humming, groaning, and tears. I now have three sons . . . and some extended time at home. I've caught up on sleep, so I'm ready.

JULY

"if he only knew what was happening in his 'opponent's' car"

Just minutes old and ready for action.

MORE AWARDS AUGUST 12, 2001

Teen Choice Awards: Los Angeles, California

This is the third year in a row I have been invited to attend the Fox Teen Choice Awards, but the it's first time I was not on tour during the date of the event. I won the Choice Extreme Athlete award last year, but never got the chance to see what the show was about. They wanted me to present the award for Choice Male Action Actor, in addition to accepting my award for this year's Choice Extreme Athlete.

A few days before the show I was faxed a copy of the script they wanted me to read, and I actually rejected it. They wanted me to say that summer action movies were "as much fun as a McTwist in a halfpipe." I thought it was cheesy, so they rewrote it and ended up giving me minimal lines. It's fun to think that I could refuse to say something that people were paid exorbitant money to write. The big buzz was that Ben Affleck won the award, and he was emerging from rehab to accept it in person. They'd stamped TOP SECRET across my script like it was a CIA document.

Justin, Tony, and Chris. Good thing they didn't ask me to harmonize.

After getting through the red carpet mayhem at the awards, I went backstage. I always like to see who I can snag pictures with behind the scenes, and I've been trying to get Britney just because she's always so aloof. She is never in the greenrooms or backstage, and rarely even in the audience. When she is around, she's flanked by at least four huge men who form an intimidation barrier. They don't want anyone getting near (or even looking at) the teenage idol. Two guys from *NSync walked by, and I assumed that they would be way too annoyed/busy/pompous to pose for a photo, but I asked anyway. Surprisingly, they were really stoked and even got one for their own collection. One of the guys supposedly dates Britney, so I guess that's the closest I'll get for now.

Erika Christensen, the girl from *Traffic,* and I were led to the stage, where I was to accept my award and we were to announce the winner. **I WAS TOLD TO KEEP IT SHORT, SO I DID. WE THEN PRESENTED BEN WITH HIS COVETED SURFBOARD TROPHY. HE BARELY ACKNOWLEDGED US, GAVE A SPEECH, AND WALKED OFFSTAGE.**

I found my seat after getting a glimpse of J-Lo preparing to go on. There were two people doing her makeup and another primping her dress as they called her to the stage. It's amazing that they didn't follow her out just in case something happened to her hair while she walked to the podium.

The rest of the show was pretty straightforward, with a few musical acts and the usual set of winners. It was good to see David Spade again. I haven't talked to him since we worked together on *Police Academy 4.* He was an avid skater in the eighties, and he still keeps up with what's happening in our world of four wheels.

Me and my copresenter, Erika Christensen. At first it was hard to shake the image of her in _Traffic,_ but she is very cool.

The handoff: Flipping a board into Andy's hand is harder than it seems.

Eric and Colin at the SportsCenter desk.

2001 SUMMER X GAMES

AUGUST 16, 2001

First Union Center: Philadelphia, Pennsylvania

I arrived late last night and spent every waking moment trying to hook up my PS2 to the hotel DSL line. I've been testing THPS3 online with the Neversoft crew almost every night lately because the game is due very soon. (The online part of THPS3 is insane, by the way.) All of my efforts were in vain— I think I forgot one adapter.

I met up with many of the other vert skaters in front of athlete registration at 8 A.M. to resolve a brewing conflict. There was a clause in the standard ESPN release form, which we all sign every year, that now gives them the right to use footage of us in an upcoming IMAX feature film about the 2001 X Games. Many of the skaters (including me) considered this unfair and thought that there should be separate deals or contracts for being included in a movie. A FEW SKATERS WHO HAVE AGENTS MANAGED TO WORK SOMETHING OUT BEFOREHAND SO THEY'D GET PAID SEPARATELY, BUT MOST WERE LEFT TO FEND FOR THEMSELVES. Max Dufor and Andy Macdonald seized the issue and formed the United Professional Skateboarders Association (UPSA) in hopes of finally getting some unity among the pros so they can bargain as a unit when it comes to some of the longstanding conflicts between the skaters and competition organizers. There was basically a forty-minute standoff in-volving a lawyer representing UPSA and various X Games representatives. The efforts were finally successful, and they removed the clause regarding the IMAX film from each skater's release form. This means that if the film-makers want to use someone's performance from the event, they would have to cut a separate deal with that skater. It was a milestone in our sport to have a group of pros stand together and actually provoke change.

Shooting for Bam's movie Haggard. I bust Ryan (center) for breaking bottles behind a store.

E 25

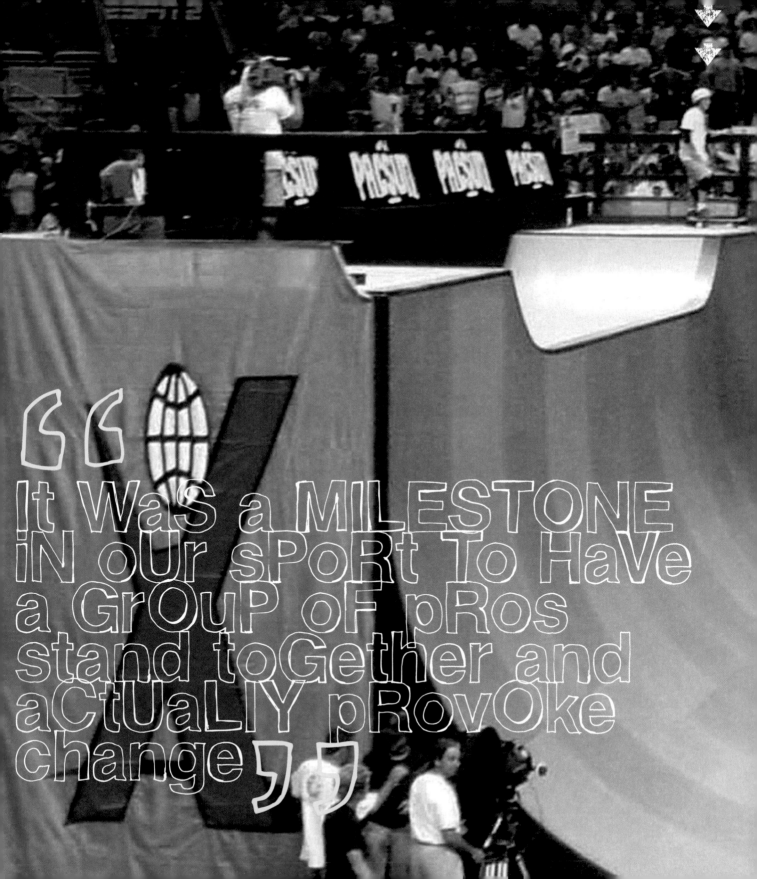

"It WaS a MILESTONE iN oUr sPoRt To HaVe a GrOuP oF pRos stand toGether and aCtUaLlY pRovoke change"

Skating makes it big time. The 2001 X Games at the 76ers' arena, Philly.

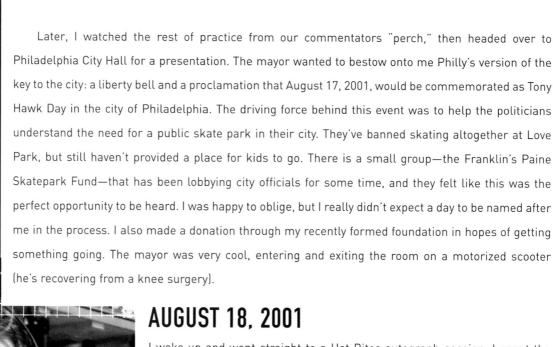

Later, I watched the rest of practice from our commentators "perch," then headed over to Philadelphia City Hall for a presentation. The mayor wanted to bestow onto me Philly's version of the key to the city: a liberty bell and a proclamation that August 17, 2001, would be commemorated as Tony Hawk Day in the city of Philadelphia. The driving force behind this event was to help the politicians understand the need for a public skate park in their city. They've banned skating altogether at Love Park, but still haven't provided a place for kids to go. There is a small group—the Franklin's Paine Skatepark Fund—that has been lobbying city officials for some time, and they felt like this was the perfect opportunity to be heard. I was happy to oblige, but I really didn't expect a day to be named after me in the process. I also made a donation through my recently formed foundation in hopes of getting something going. The mayor was very cool, entering and exiting the room on a motorized scooter (he's recovering from a knee surgery).

AUGUST 18, 2001

I woke up and went straight to a Hot Bites autograph session. I spent the next two hours at the Verizon Wireless store trying to resolve cellular problems. If it's not the phone, then it's the service that causes me eternal grief. They ended up replacing my phone after all that time, but I left to find that the roaming service was not set up properly. I couldn't stand to sit in the dungeon-esque service room any longer, so I gave up and decided to survive the week sans Motorola.

Not internationally known, but known to rock a microphone.

The first controversy for the skate events reared its ugly head when Renton Millar got injured and was unable to compete in the finals. World Cup (the skate event organizer) have allowed the next qualifier in previous contests to replace the injured skater so that they'll have a ten-man final, but set a precedent earlier this year by only allowing those who qualified. This was to insure that the absent skater still gets tenth place and is considered a finalist. Neal Hendrix (the eleventh-place qualifier) offered to take his eleventh-place prize money if he would be allowed to skate in the finals, regardless of whether his placing improved at the end. They decided to stick to the rule book for the sake of consistency. The rules have been bent in the past and they did not want any more complaints of favoritism or selective enforcement. Nine skaters in the finals—case closed.

The vert finals got off to a slow start, with almost everyone bailing on his first two runs. The third runs were a different story—highlights include Tas Pappas's incredible five-trick combo of kickflip Indy / varial kickflip Indy / varial kickflip Indy 360 / 720 / frontside 540. The rest of his run was not as technical, but solid. He apparently didn't like his score and gave an interview of three words to Jason Ellis: "The judging sucks." Andy Mac had a jam-packed run, pulling off a varial five, a barrage of nollie heelflips, and a nollie frontside five. I felt the scoring was especially low for him, because every wall of his run was a difficult trick. Bucky made an all-time run, only falling on a switch five at the end. Bob Burnquist was the last skater and he did what only Bob can do—possibly the best vert run ever, including a switch kickflip Indy, switch kickflip Indy to fakie (grabbing dark side by accident and flopping it over), switch hurricane, half-Cab to frontside blunt, and a blunt kickflip to fakie as a cherry on top. I was so fired up that my headset fell off while I was jumping around and I had to retrieve it just to yell into the microphone, "Blunt kickflip to fakie! Blunt kickflip to fakie!" It was the run of a lifetime. Even if Tas had scored higher, I think he would still have ended up in third just behind Bucky and Bob.

"the mayor was very cool, entering and exiting the room on a motorized scooter."

AUGUST 19, 2001

Andy and I always try to skate together for at least a couple of days to work out lines for the doubles event. But then we always decide to change it the day of the event because the ramp might be different or because we figure out something that works better. The hardest thing is distinguishing the lines from each other, and not forgetting where to be on what wall. ONE SLIGHT MISTAKE COULD MEAN A NASTY COLLISION, AND WE'VE HAD OUR SHARE. WE WORKED OUT OUR LINES FOR TWO HOURS AND SEEMED TO GET THEM DIALED.

Just as we were to get started, another controversy came up to bite World Cup. Bob had chosen Jen (his girlfriend) as his partner, but the rulebook (dating back to 1998) states that both competitors must be qualified for the X Games. Everyone thought it was cool that they were going to skate together, but there were grumblings that some skaters would have picked other partners knowing that they could choose someone outside the list of prequalified skaters. For the sake of consistency, World Cup stuck to their guidelines and did not allow them to skate in the event. They were allowed a "demo run" before the contest got started, but were not scored. It should be made clear that these are not issues with ESPN, but with the appointed event organizers. ESPN will honor what the World Cup panel decides—they have no advantage either way. I hoped they would allow Bob and Jen to skate officially, for the sake of getting some girls in the mix, but I understood the precedent.

"we had an idea to try some sort of transfer where I did a 900 over Andy if things were looking good at the end"

Everything went well for Andy and me—we made both runs exactly as planned. We had an idea to try some sort of transfer where I did a 900 over Andy if things were looking good at the end. I spun a few just before our last run, trying to get a feel for it. Our last run was exactly what we wanted it to be, so we paused on the deck and decided to go for it. I was pretty winded, but I thought I could muster up the energy for one last trick. I was doomed from my first setup air because I landed too low, so I tried to force it. My spin didn't make up for the lack of height, but I tried to put it on the wall anyway. I ended up shooting out and falling straight on my hip, but I was happy to get that close. Other highlights were Chris Gentry and Mike Crum making up a line during practice and pulling the whole thing when it counted, and Bucky and Matt Dove skating as the "Baltimorons" with their helmets on backward.

A 540 over a tailslide, feeble under a backside air. The key to doubles is to be in the right place at the right time, no matter what.

147

"We'd like you to sign a few things before you go."

AUGUST 20, 2001

Again, went straight from bed to the venue for the "park" event (formerly known as street). By the time it got started, I realized that my commentating gig during this event was going to cut into my practice for best trick (which I decided to enter just before heading to Philly), so I only helped announce the first runs.

I only had two tricks planned for best trick—if I could make them both early on, then I was going to try some kickflip fives. I wanted to do a 360 ollie to boardslide (which I recently learned) and a varial heelflip lien 360 (which I've only done twice) before trying anything else. The format was supposed to be a twenty-minute jam, but we convinced them to extend it to thirty (and hoped to get more if something was going down). I pulled the first trick after a few tries, just after Bob landed a fakie to fakie heelflip Indy 540. Tas tried a few 900s, but was nearly hanging up on the coping every time. Matt Dove was wearing a shirt that read EXTREME $ PROFIT NETWORK (for ESPN). He evidently was having a bad experience in Philly with regard to ESPN and wanted to make a statement about small prize money and better treatment for the skaters. Anyway, Matt spent the entire jam trying Indy varial 720s. My second trick was giving me more trouble than I had expected, and I tried it up past the thirty-minute mark. Dave Duncan, old-school skateboarder/skateboard judge/announcer/skatepark designer and builder, announced that we could have a few more minutes, and I ended up making one. BOB ALSO PULLED A SWITCH KICKFLIP INDY 360, WHERE HE CAUGHT IT HALFWAY AND ROLLED IT ONTO HIS FEET IN TRUE BOB FASHION. IT WAS THE BEST TRICK BY FAR. I started trying something that I had just thought of in practice (a frontside fakie to fakie varial five), but it seemed like it was going to be too much effort and there was not enough time to see it to completion. I distinctly heard Duncan count down the event and thank all of the pros for giving it their all. I decided to try a 900 to appease the forty thousand-plus spectators, many of whom expected to see me do it. I knew the contest was officially over, and didn't want to try to re-create the 1999 event, anyway. I was happy just to try it for the audience. Soon after,

"Can I borrow your pen?"

Matt landed his trick and I assumed it didn't count. I tried to stick a 900 and came down *hard* on the same hip I'd injured the day before. It hurt a lot. I got up and my leg was stinging from my hip down, but I had enough to give it another try. I refused to fall again the same way, because it would have definitely taken me out of commission. I spun faster than ever and nailed a good one to an appreciative audience. In my rejoicing, I noticed a drama start to unfold on the flat bottom.

Matt Dove had been informed that his trick did not count within the time limit, and that Bob was going to be awarded first place. There was some confusion as to whether the time was extended up until the end, but I definitely heard them count it down beforehand. Matt was under the impression that because he'd worn the anti-ESPN shirt and had chosen to speak his opinion, he was being singled out and would be excluded from the programming of the event. He went and

"i got up and my leg was stinging from my hip down, but I had enough to give it another try"

Ellis interviews Matt Dove about his controversial shirt.

stood on the winners' podium, claiming that he should have won and that not allowing his trick to count was another example of all the favoritism and improper tactics employed at these events. What he was failing to realize was that the issue was not with ESPN, but (again) with World Cup sticking to their rules. After 1999, they decided that tricks landed after the official time limit expired were not to be counted. I never expected them to count my 900 that year, but the skaters unanimously decided to give it to me. Matt was claiming that he would have never kept trying it if he knew the time was up.

I WAS UNDER *THE* IMPRESSION THAT HE ENJOYED PUSHING THE LIMITS AND WANTED TO LAND ONE FOR HIMSELF—THE VERY REASON MOST OF US CHOSE SKATING IN THE FIRST PLACE. In fact, most of us wanted

Matt to make it during the time frame and take the win properly. I went down and tried to explain to

him that although he had some valid points—about the need for bigger prize money and more equitable treatment for the athletes—they had nothing to do with this particular issue. He then told me that if certain "other" skaters had landed a trick after time, it would definitely count because they are the bigger names and the ones ESPN likes to cover (meaning Bob, Bucky, and me). They would bend the rules if we played nice, so to speak. I told him that they certainly didn't do Bob any favors by prohibiting Jen and him from skating doubles, and I saw a glimmer of reasoning in his face, but not for long. He was convinced that ESPN would "lose" the footage of him landing the trick just to sweep it under the rug. I knew this wouldn't be the case—he had one of the best tricks and they would definitely want to show it on the air (even if it didn't count).

Matt cites other times the rules have been bent to World Cup organizer Don Bostick.

Suddenly there were cameras surrounding our argument, and I was feeling like he wanted to make an example out of me when in reality I simply wanted to point out that this was a separate issue from the one he was initially protesting. World Cup decides the winner, not ESPN. It was very sad to see such a great display of skating soured by misguided frustration. Surprisingly, World Cup decided to give him the medal. Ironically, this was the first time that World Cup bent their rules during the entire X Games—exactly what Matt was supposedly protesting—perhaps because he wouldn't leave the winner's podium. This was my final comment on this situation: I pulled a varial 720 before I made the 900 in the 1999 X Games Best Trick competition. The judges considered a 900 the "best trick" out of the two. If Matt's Indy varial 720 at this year's contest counted after the jam had ended, then why wouldn't my 900, which I made just after Matt made his 720, also count?

The saddest part of the whole situation is that Matt has some valid points about prize money and treatment of the athletes, and I totally agree with him on those. But this was not the forum for those complaints. I don't think it was an effective protest and actually made the programming worse for what could have been a great event to see on television. The fans missed out in the end.

Bob, Andy, and I discuss something very important, like which wall is best for 540s.

POST 9/11 SEPTEMBER 15, 2001

Shaqtacular: Los Angeles, California

Less than a week after the day of terror, tragedy, and unforgivable acts of evil, Shaquille O'Neal had the courage to carry on his annual fund-raiser: Shaqtacular, a benefit for AEFK (Athletes and Entertainers for Kids). I had wondered if it would still be held, privately hoping all along that it would. Terrorism cannot stop us from living our lives, and it must not stop us from helping our children. I was invited early on in the planning of this event and I refused to cancel my participation because of looming fears of more attacks. I had no idea what to expect, but I imagined the mood would be somber.

John, my nephew and trusty celebrity-event companion, joined me for the drive to Universal CityWalk and managed to tolerate my sudden addiction to AM news radio (to hear updates on the terrorist probe). We arrived on time, got shuffled through a random kitchen, and ended up in a check-in room. I didn't recognize anybody there, but John could pick out at least half of the guests as television personalities. I don't get to watch too much network TV these days, so I'm out of the loop. As we emerged into the "playfield," I recognized a few guests: Damon Wayans, David Arquette, and Tom Arnold. I was assigned to a team of four "athletes" consisting of Malik from the latest version of *The Real World*, and a girl and a guy, both of whom appeared to be actors. We were so rushed into the opening ceremonies that we didn't have time for formal introductions.

The concept of this fund-raiser is to have eight teams of four participate in fabricated activities that combine traditional sports and random obstacles. There were points given for making it around each obstacle and for number of goals scored. Shaq was the captain for the Vons/Coca-Cola team, and it was obvious that he was determined to take his team to victory (mostly by cheating and disrupting other teams' performances). Money is raised by charging huge ticket prices a thousand dollars each) for spectators to get close to the celebrities and witness their antics. There were also food kiosks and autograph booths if the paying public got bored of the pseudo–sporting events.

The event began with short speeches by the organizers and major contributors, and then the big guy grabbed the microphone. He called for a moment of silence to remember the victims. I realized

that up until that point, the event had been relatively joyful and not the awkward grief-stricken gathering that I had envisioned. With that, he thanked everyone for their participation and introduced Jessica Simpson, who belted out a heartfelt rendition of the national anthem. Her tight sweatpants were on the verge of falling down toward the end of her performance, forcing her to keep pulling them up with one hand. I can guarantee that almost every guy there was watching her underwear as it made a brief cameo onstage. She finished without (major) incident, and the guests were called onto the court/stage/field to participate in a TaeBo warmup session led by Billy Blanks, the self-proclaimed master of the latest exercise craze. He led the group as if we were all regulars in his class, and I now believe that he was on a mission to humiliate as many celebrities as possible. I kept up as best I could, and even broke out in a sweat near the end. Whatever the intention, we were warmed up by default.

THE "GAMES" BEGAN WITH THE SOCCER RELAY AND QUICKLY MOVED TO OTHER WACKY EVENTS, SUCH AS THE FOOTBALL FRENZY AND THE BASKETBALL BATTLE.

After the terrorist attacks back east, we need events like Shaq's to help each other and to distract ourselves from worrying too much. I will never stop asking why these recent tragic events took place, but getting out and returning to some sense of normalcy made me realize that life must go on and we should embrace it, now more than ever.

Malik and I rejoicing in the fact that Shaq didn't squash us.

"
we need events like Shaq's to help each other and to distract ourselves from worrying too much "

155

My first and last experience with Tae Bo.

NOVEMBER 6, 2001

I was originally flying to New York City on November 7, but couldn't pass up the offer to hitch a ride on a private jet with Bobby Kotick—Activision's CEO. It is an incredible experience—no check-in, no gates, no disgruntled employees, and no risk of terrorist activities (OK, very little). The plane picked me up at the Carlsbad airport, where I literally drove onto the runway to meet it. A crew of three (pilot, co-pilot, and Citation representative) greeted me, we got on, and that was it for the boarding process. The pilot looked back from the cockpit, asked if we were ready, and we were off to Van Nuys to pick up Bobby. I feel eternally spoiled for air travel from this point on—it feels more like carpooling than mass transit. After a half-hour "layover" in Van Nuys, Bobby and his father-in-law joined us and we were off to the Big Apple. On the way, I learned that the Citation jet we were riding in is the fastest private jet available—the pilot said he's made it from Los Angeles to New York in less than four hours with good tailwinds. It's not the roomiest—there were only eight seats—but they were plush. IT WAS LIKE A COZY LIVING ROOM. THERE WAS A BOOMING AUDIO-VIDEO SYSTEM AND CATERED FOOD. I FEEL LIKE I WAS OFFERED A PEEK INTO A DOORWAY OF EXTRAVAGANCE THAT I DON'T WANT TO CLOSE.

NOVEMBER 7, 2001

New York City

This was the day I was originally supposed to fly in, so I didn't have too many commitments. I vowed to visit Ground Zero at some point in the day, so I had lunch with Renee (my book editor) and made my way toward Soho to visit Sarah Hall Productions and get closer to the damage. It was starting to get dark as I walked toward the financial district and The Smell began to hit me. It is a combination of dust, must, ash, and the unspeakable. I passed dozens of people in surgical and gas masks and realized that they have been working in this environment every day. I finally came to numerous barricades and fences surrounding the area of the former Twin Towers. The crews have done an incredible job of containing the damage of the two collapsed 110-story buildings and blocking the general public from all of the mayhem. I saw the remnants of a few buildings—barely standing with seven stories of destroyed furniture, paperwork, and walls piled in between. The television coverage does it no justice—it is a massive, chaotic, dangerous graveyard that looks impossible to clean or make any sense of. **TO A VISITOR, NEW YORKERS SEEMED TO BE BACK IN TERMS OF OPTIMISM AND WORK ROUTINES.** Staying uptown, you'd never know that anything happened. Until, of course, you pass a fire station and see the hordes of flowers, messages, and prayers that adorn their entrances and honor their fallen brothers. CNN can't provide the emotional impact of being there and seeing it for yourself. I tried to sort through the many feelings that I had encountered on my pilgrimage, but never came to any conclusions.

"I tried to sort through the many feelings that I had encountered on my pilgrimage, but never came to any conclusions"

E25

WTC: Aftermath and remembrance.

NOVEMBER 9, 2001

New York City to Houston, Texas

Woke up early to make a morning meeting with ESPN to discuss the Gigantic Skatepark Tour for summer 2002. If we do it, it will probably be the last one—I don't want it to become stagnant and too formulaic. I really want to take it beyond the mainland United States, to places like Hawaii or Alaska, or even international locations like Australia or Brazil. This, of course, will be determined by the budget we are allowed and will be decided at a much later date. At least I got to plant the seed.

Riley boardslides the long rail. Gigantic Skatepark Tour, Jacksonville, FL, 2002.

These types of displays are very strange to me.

HAWK STORE #2

DECEMBER 8, 2001

Hawk Store Grand Opening: Salt Lake City, Utah

After much debate, I finally convinced Erin to take a trip with me—she has refused to fly since September 11, but this short trip was the perfect reintroduction to air travel. I scrambled to make overnight arrangements for Spencer, and Aunt Lolo, thankfully, came to the rescue. We (Erin, Keegan, my sister Pat, and Jared) landed in Salt Lake City just before 2 P.M. It seems that they are quickly trying to give the city a facelift in time for the highly anticipated 2002 Winter Olympics crowds. The Gateway Shopping Center is further proof of this update—a new, sophisticated mall with plenty of shops to please the younger crowd (Bebe, Abercrombie & Fitch, J. Crew, Barnes & Noble, California Pizza Kitchen, Ruby's, and a Mega-Plex Theatre). Included in all of this is the second Hawk Skate store, located right next to a Boardrider's Club. The store had already been open for a while, but they wanted to have it running smoothly before doing an "official" opening.

THE STORE HAD A RAFFLE WITH THREE HUNDRED WINNERS SO THAT THE CROWD WOULDN'T GET OUT OF HAND AS IT DID DURING THE NEW JERSEY OPENING.

I made it through the line in about two hours, and signed for another hundred or so people who just showed up (nonwinners). Erin and Keegan braved the ferocious winter cold (OK, so we're from Southern California) and managed to do some much-needed Christmas shopping while I sat and signed away. Keegan experienced his first flight and first encounter with snow in the same day.

Keegan's introduction to air travel.

MY NOTE
TH

7

163

DECEMBER 9, 2001

Our original plan was to hit a local skatepark before our flight home, but the weather had covered all the outdoor parks in snow and the indoor park sounded too chilly. Jared and I took up a snowboarding offer and headed to Park City. It was the best conditions they've had in years. I rode until my legs were too wobbly, managing to find some short, untracked powder runs near the top. It was the best day of riding I've had in a long time, and it required the least amount of preparation.

We headed down the mountain in time to meet Erin and Keegan, check out of the hotel, get some food, and make our flight home. The one crowd we didn't encounter during this trip was the one we expected most—at the security checkpoint. The airport looked to be running like it did before September 11 (which may not be a good thing) but we were early to the gate for a change. Our short flight seemed much longer, as Keegan was not happy most of the way unless one of us was walking the aisle while holding him. The journey from the front of the plane to the rear and back again gets old fast.

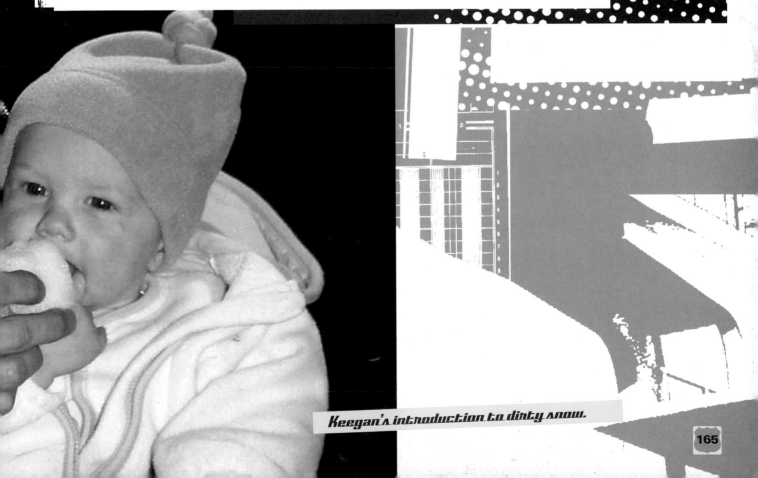

Keegan's introduction to dirty snow.

"I rode until my legs were too wobbly"

A 540 in the deep end of the Park City skatepark, Park City, UT.

Acknowledgments

Thanks to Erin, Riley, Spencer, and Keegan; Mom and Eric; Lenore, Dick, Greg, and John; Pat, Alan, Hagen, and Emily; Steve, Pamm, Will, and Cameron. All at THI, SHP, WMA, Slam, Blitz, 900, Hawk, Quik, Atlas, Activision, Neversoft, BSP, Rebel Waltz, TWS, Big Brother, Slap, ESPN, Redline, Heinz, TSG, Arnette, Mainframe, Nixon, Apple, and all my friends that will hopefully forgive me for not listing them.

More titles from

—TONY HAWK —

HAWK
Occupation: Skateboarder
ISBN 0-06-095831-6 (paperback)

In his bestselling adult autobiography, Tony Hawk, a.k.a "The Birdman," shares the events that have influenced his life, skateboarding's history, and his rise to becoming a skateboarding legend. His story is a touching tale of perseverance and determination. Despite the ups and downs in his career, his dedication has made him a skateboarding god and a hero to Generation X.

"All the raw tales about bodily functions, smashing junk cars and setting oneself on fire that you might expect from a veteran skateboarder." —*Wall Street Journal*

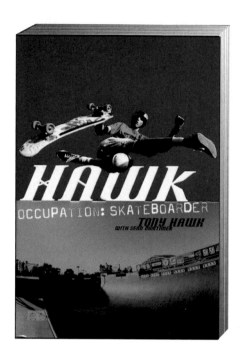

TONY HAWK
Professional Skateboarder
ISBN 0-06-009689-6 (paperback)

Tony Hawk has rewritten his autobiography with his younger fans in mind. A gifted, hyper, supercompetitive "demon" child who found peace while on a skateboard, Tony was teased by classmates and harassed by his competitors. Instead of looking to violence or finding comfort in drugs, he practiced even more. Tony's story offers young adults inspiration to stand up for what they believe in, and illustrates that sometimes the "losers" can finish first.

"An inside look at the molding of a great role model— there's so much more than just the 900!"
—Bob Burnquist, world champion skater